Lead On!

The Complete Handbook
for Group Leaders

Leslie Griffin Lawson

Franklyn D. Donant

and John D. Lawson

Impact ✇ Publishers
POST OFFICE BOX 1094
SAN LUIS OBISPO, CALIFORNIA 93406

Library of Congress Cataloging in Publication Data

Lawson, Leslie Griffin, 1946-
    Lead on!

    Includes bibliographical references and index.
    1. Leadership.   2. Voluntarism.   3. Small groups.
4. Interpersonal relations.   I. Donant, Franklyn D.
II. Lawson, John D.   III. Title.
HMI4I.L37   1982   303.3'4   82-15553
ISBN 0-915166-27-5 (pbk.)

PUBLISHER'S NOTE
This publication is designed to provide accurate and authoritative information in regard to the subject matter covered. It is sold with the understanding that the publisher is not engaged in rendering psychological, medical, or other professional services. If expert assistance or counseling is needed, the services of a competent professional should be sought.

Illustrated by Steve Austin

Printed in the United States of America

Published by *Impact ⟨⟩ Publishers*
POST OFFICE BOX 1094
SAN LUIS OBISPO, CALIFORNIA 93406

ARE YOU READY TO LEAD?

This Table of CONTENTS will help you to decide…

Lead On!

Volunteerism, participation, cooperation, equality: basic American ethics.

Volunteerism in America is a way of life, our trademark, what we're all about. We learn it culturally because it's all around us. We offer help, give time, step forward without being asked. And we start and join volunteer groups and organizations throughout the land to do it bigger and better.

Volunteers were the pioneers, the adventurers, the experimenters who took Robert Frost's "untraveled road." And, truly, that *has* made all the difference.

Today, the volunteer spirit is not only alive and well, it is an increasing force in raising the quality of life throughout the world, a blessing to those in need, a collective voice in bringing about change, and a major influence in our daily lives when the work is done.

As public funds become less and less available to meet the needs of the disadvantaged and to provide so-called "non-essential" programs, the spirit of volunteerism rises again to feed, to comfort, and to nurture. In community service, in health care, in the arts, in education, in environmental protection, in nutrition, in crisis intervention, in programs for young and old, for black and brown and red and white and yellow, for men and for women — it is *volunteers* who are making things happen.

Organizations born of this enterprising and lusty heritage range from simple to complex, from transient to indestructible, and from ultra informal to the American Academy of Parliamentarians. Some have large professional staffs, multi-million dollar budgets, and thousands of volunteers to accomplish their lofty missions. Others have no staff at all; they collect membership dues, sponsor fund-raising drives, and fill a need.

Every volunteer group has one very important strength: people who are attracted to it *arrive* motivated. They come because they *value* what the group stands for, and because they want to contribute to its success.

In order to retain that enthusiasm, every volunteer organization must keep its machinery in order (membership, leadership, relationships, and resources). Leaders must involve every willing participant in setting and achieving organizational goals, and must tend to the needs of the members themselves as well.

And *that,* fellow volunteers, is what this book is all about.

Having a Great Year

From the first day of your leadership experience, you will do well to realize that there is no way you can have a great year by doing everything yourself. Nor will it be a great year if you enlist the help only of a few of your ''cronies,'' or even those tried-and-true members who did it all last year.

A great year is the product of skillful leadership, which includes:

- Letting every member feel that you know s/he is there, and that you believe each person ''owns just as much stock'' in the organization as you do;
- Applying some basic group skills to enhance membership participation and involvement; and
- Being sensitive and understanding enough to use these group processes in such a way that things keep moving toward the goals of the members, and at a pace that makes them feel they are personally getting something out of their involvement.

LEAD ON! is dedicated to the proposition that every volunteer group leader deserves to have a truly great year, every year. And we predict *you* will, too...if you study and practice the 24 key leadership skills presented informally and straightforwardly in the pages that follow.

Part 1

"Tuning Up"

Effective leadership depends on understanding and caring about yourself and other people. That's why these basics are presented in the first four chapters.

- Understanding your own leadership style and how it affects others.
- Knowing what is important to your members, so you can keep them motivated.
- Being able to express your ideas and feelings to others and to understand the messages they send to you.
- Recognizing and responding sensitively to the special needs of members of varied backgrounds.

(HINT: The rest of *LEAD ON!* is built on these foundations/)
READ ON!!

1

Understanding Your Own Leadership Style

When it comes to being an effective leader, some folks seem to have "it," others don't. And although "it" is difficult to define in specific terms, we generally know "it" when we see "it." Take, for example, the following pairs of characters seen regularly on commercial TV:

M*A*S*H* (reruns)	Colonel Potter	Major Burns
Mary Tyler Moore	Mary Richards	Ted Baxter
Muppets	Kermit-the-Frog	Miss Piggy
Happy Days	Arthur Fonzarelli	Ralph Malph
Barney Miller	Captain Miller	Inspector Luger

In a very general and stereotypical way, each of these sets contains one fictional character who has a positive, productive influence on others, and a second character who (alas) bungles repeatedly in trying to establish mutually satisfying relationships with friends and colleagues.

Leadership may be defined as "...A process of influencing others toward setting goals and achieving them. Consider these other historical and current examples of people reputed to have "it" in the public arena (regardless of whether you identify *at all* with their politics, methods, or goals!): Martin Luther King, Lech Walesa, John F. Kennedy, Golda Maier, Fidel Castro, John Wooden, Jane Fonda, Jesse Jackson, Winston Churchill, Eva Peron.

Some would say that such leaders are "born that way," that they had certain personality traits that made them "naturals" for assuming positions of leadership in modern society. It is reasonable to believe that some people may have a head start on effective leadership due to a combination of hereditary and environmental factors. However, *way* too much emphasis has been put on in-born personal traits. Much more often than not, *leaders are made, not born.* What does the trick is simply learning and practicing a set of skills, including awareness of and responsiveness to the needs, values, and interests of members, and helping move a group toward achieving its goals. People who have "it" enable others to strike a balance between the human and task dimensions of working together.

You can have "it," too, if you pay close attention to how what you do affects the behavior of your membership. That's exactly what this chapter is all about.

Leadership is an interactive process, and no matter what the leader does, the members will react. The real key to effective leadership is to be able to accurately assess what the members need from you *at any point in time,* and to be able to tailor your style to those needs.

Research on this topic has found that *interactive leadership* has three parts:

1. *Task Behavior:* Emphasis the leader puts on organizing members and defining their roles and the procedures they should follow to get the job done;

2. *Relationship Behavior:* Emphasis the leader puts on maintaining positive feelings; giving members support, encouragement, information, and rewards;

3. *The Situation* in which the group is operating. The single most important aspect of any leadership situation is the collective "personality" of the membership, which can range from highly informed, motivated and capable (mature), to uninformed, unsure, organizationally naive, and not familiar with the work that needs to be done (immature).

The best leadership style depends upon how "mature" the members are, and that will vary from task to task.

An example may be helpful. Let's say you are president of the Harmer Valley P.T.A., which for the past ten years has sponsored an annual carnival. People are excited about the event, the committees are well established and the chairpersons know what they're doing. You assess the maturity of the group in relation to this particular project, and can establish fairly easily that they're highly mature. What's your choice of leadership style? Low Task/Low Relationship. How should you behave? Step back, delegate, and let them get the job done! They're well equipped to handle it with only minimal assistance and support from you.

Let's take the same organization, now, but look at a different task that needs to be done: rewriting the 42-page by-laws (yech...). The by-laws have not been rewritten since they were first drafted 25 years ago. Although you have a committee in place to work on them, the Chair isn't real excited at the prospect of being responsible for this humongous job, and the other two members are brand new to the group. Maturity level? Clearly low. The style you need to use? High Task/Low Relationship. How should you behave? Get together regularly (weekly, if necessary) with the Chair and give a lot of assistance. Review the history of the organization, help draw up an outline of the new by-laws, set a deadline for the first draft to be done, and keep in close touch in case of snags along the way. In short, be highly directive and specific, and keep focusing on the task at hand.

Here is a "shorthand prescription" for which style to employ:

task-maturity	appropriate leadership style
Low	High Task/Low Relationship ("Telling")
Low-moderate	High Task/High Relationship ("Selling")
High-moderate	High Relationship/Low Task ("Participating")
High	Low Relationship/Low Task ("Delegating")

As member task-maturity increases, the leader should reduce emphasis on task, and increase emphasis on relationships. When members become moderately task-mature, slowly let them go on their own. They'll be ready to give *each other* the support and encouragement they need!

The key to applying the right style at the right time, of course, is knowing a lot about the people in your organization: their skills and abilities, interests, likes and dislikes. (See Chapters 7 and 8 for ways to become more adept at this.) And, while it's not often possible to exactly pinpoint their maturity level on a given task, the better you know them the closer you'll come to being accurate with your "ballpark guesstimates." Practice makes perfect, and over time you'll find that pausing briefly to do a quick maturity assessment before launching into a project will pay off many times over in member satisfaction and productivity (as well as leader energy savings!). Why get in there and mess around with getting things done when they're better off without you?

Here are a few other payoffs for adjusting your style to respond appropriately to the membership:
• When you relate to people as individuals, and give them credit for their competence and experience, their good feelings about you and the group increase. They become more active, loyal members.
• Interactive leadership encourages people to learn, develop their skills and move into positions of responsibility more quickly than if they are always closely supervised and told what to do. While you may get acceptable short-term results with a directive and structured approach to leadership, the long-term effects are likely to be negative, especially with mature members in the group.
• When members get the assistance they need without having to scrounge for it on their own, they'll be able to move ahead confidently. In leader-dominated groups, many potential leaders are discouraged from participating fully. They believe they don't know enough about an office or a project to get involved, and they're afraid to ask for information or to volunteer to help.

• This approach encourages freedom, initiative, and creativity among those who are given a job to do. If people have to wait to be told what to do before they're able to act, projects will bog down when you're out of town (or out to lunch). The more you give away to mature members, the more time you'll have to help those who really need you.

Before leaving the topic of leadership styles, a few words contrasting *effective* with *successful* leadership are in order. If Sadie wants Sam to do something, her leadership attempt can be considered to be *successful* if she can just get Sam to complete the task. *But,* if Sadie's style is not compatible with Sam's expectations of his leader, and if Sam is angry afterwards and only did the job because Sadie exerted her power and made him feel guilty, Sadie has been *successful*, but not *effective.*

Success is measured by how the group or individual actually behaves when asked to do something. Effectiveness is measured not only in terms of *task* accomplishment, but also by how the members *feel* about the process. Effectiveness results when leaders have the sensitivity to know what members want and need, and, in a conscious, careful way, are able to deliver those behaviors required to facilitate group productivity. By being "adjustable" and consistent about employing the different styles needed for different situations, the behavior of the leader becomes highly predictable and a source of comfort and enjoyment for the members of the organization.

And, speaking of the wants and needs of members, let us introduce a friend of ours, Hapathy Jones. "Hap" will be our companion in the next chapter as we explore ways to "turn members on" by meeting *their* needs.

O.K., all you *effective* leaders: READ ON!!

For Further Reading

• Francis, Dave and Young, Doug, *Improving Work Groups: A Practical Manual for Team Building.* San Diego, CA: University Associates, 1979, pp. 154-159.

• Gibb, J.R., Platts, Grace N. and Miller, Lorraine I., *Dynamics of Participative Groups.* St. Louis, MO: John S. Swift Co., 1951, pp. 16-21.
  A pragmatic presentation of autocratic, permissive, and participative structures and styles. Participative action motivates, leads to personal development, produces realistic decisions, enhances interpersonal relations, and is an experience in democratic ethics.

• Harris, Thomas A., *I'm Ok — You're Ok: A Practical Guide to Transactional Analysis.* New York: Harper and Row Publishers, 1969.
  A mental health model of interpersonal relations based upon TA's four possible combinations of me and you. Clear implications for four leadership styles.

• Hersey, Paul and Blanchard, Kenneth H., *Management of Organizational Behavior: Utilizing Human Resources.* Englewood Cliffs, NJ: Prentice-Hall, Inc., 1977.
  A model of interpersonal behavior based upon the difficulty of the task, and the nature of leader-member relationships. Both affect the member's skill level and commitment. This model is used in this chapter.

• McGregor, Douglas, *The Human Side of Enterprise.* New York: McGraw-Hill Book Company, 1960.
  Based on management of human resources in business and industry, this book advances the merit of theory "Y." Assumes positive characteristics in people, integrates individual and organizational goals, presents leadership as a relationship, and stresses participation and collaboration.

• Pfeiffer, J. William and Jones, John E. (Eds.), "Styles of leadership: A series of role plays." La Jolla, CA: University Associates, *A Handbook of Structured Experiences for Human Relations Training,* Volume V, 1975, pp. 19-33.
  Explores impact of leaders on decision making groups; demonstrates effects of hidden agendas.

- Steers, Richard M., *Introduction to Organizational Behavior.* Santa Monica, CA: Goodyear Publishing Co., Inc., 1981.

Business management principles applied to volunteer organizations, particularly leadership and group effectiveness.

- Wood, Julia T., "Leadership as persuasion and adaptation." La Jolla, CA: University Associates, *Annual Handbook for Group Facilitators, 1976,* pp. 132-135.*

Offers a realistic and useful means for understanding how leaders emerge, maintain their power, and build effective, cohesive groups.

---

* University Associates' *Annual Handbook for Group Facilitators* is such a recurring resource for us, we have elected to abbreviate its entries in this book. Bibliographies in later chapters will refer to the *Handbook* as "AHGF" together with the year of publication.

2
Motivating Members

"If it weren't for my apathetic membership, I'd be doing
fine! I guess that's just the way it is these days with volunteers — they just don't give a damn!"

Sorry, Charlie. Membership apathy is more likely to be a
result of the leader's inappropriate style or lack of understanding than something insidious, evil, or lazy in members,
as tough as that may be for many leaders to accept.

Apathy is no more and no less than the "flipside" of motivation. An apathetic member is in a state of equilibrium...
unconcerned, placid, satisfied, and without emotion...
unaware of the "turn-on" opportunities that surround
him/her...burdened with a low self-concept or with little hope
of success...immobilized by fear of failure and unwilling to
take risks...characterized by such excuses as "I'm not interested," "I don't have the time," "I'd love to, but...."

A "wise old owl" is credited with this definition: "*Apathy*
is an infectious disease of the ear. People get *apathy* from
being constantly subjected to the oral pronouncements of
leaders who talk too much." In advanced stages, this infec-
tion destroys a member's "turn-on valve" and *ZAP!* Another
active member drops out of sight.

Every leader is faced with the problem of how to motivate
members: how to get them to do what needs to be done...or at
least to *do something*.

If you're like most leaders, Hapathy Jones is probably one
of your typical members. Like you and me, "Hap" carries
four things with him at all times...his *values,* his *needs,* his
interests and his *self-concept.* No one can see these things,
but they're there. How did Hap acquire his unique collection
of these attributes? Well, it's a pretty complex process, because they are all interrelated, so we'll take them one at a
time.

Values

Hap's *values* are deep-rooted principles and beliefs that have formed continuously since he was a child. They come from the influence of close associations with family, very special friends, and people Hap wanted to be like. Some folks have developed very strong values, and change them little throughout life. Others slip and slide a bit more in relation to their values, depending on what kind of opportunities are presented to them.

Values influence all personal decisions to some extent: choosing close friends, deciding how to use leisure time, determining what organizations to join or activities to pursue within those organizations — all these decisions tie back to the things people value. People also must choose *between* values from time to time when they are in conflict...like deciding to tell a lie (when they really do value honesty) in order to keep a friend out of trouble (because they place a high value on friendship). Tough choices, those.

Needs

Hap experiences stress when something is lacking in his life or environment. This stress creates a *need,* which in turn moves him to seek relief or satisfaction. It's like the stress your body feels when you need food, water, or comfort and you, in turn, act to satisfy those needs.

Stress also develops when members feel the need to have a favorable self-image, positive notice from others, feelings of certainty, a sense of belonging, or new experiences. All of us are likely to move toward those experiences that promise fulfillment, and a reduction in stress.

Interests

Hap's feelings of curiosity, attentiveness, and excitement are called *interests.* They can be life-long, such as hobbies and recreational pursuits, or they can be temporary and take the form of fads, styles, or whims.

Self-Concept

Finally, Hap has a very personal feeling about himself, which is made up of his overall perception of his image, his worthiness, his *self-concept.* It's a self-portrait of what he believes himself to be, based upon self-observations (and feedback from others) in many different situations. This underlying sense of self is very much a part of Hap when he faces new situations. If he sees himself as inept at expressing himself in meetings, for instance, he may withhold ideas and information that could be helpful to the group. Or, if he had a lousy experience as an officer of some other organization, he is likely to be unexcited about trying it again.

So here's Hap: someone you really know very little about, but someone you really want to motivate as a member of your organization. What can be done?

First, get his attention. Make him aware of something you want him to do. Write different projects or opportunities on a chalkboard, plaster them on newsprint, or go for the big time and use a projector. Ask Hap and other members to talk about these options for involvement in small groups, and then extol the wondrous beauty and variety of it all!

However hard you try to get him interested, the decision about involvement will be Hap's, not yours. He'll be asking himself (at some level), "Is this activity compatible with my values, needs and interests?" and "Is it achievable?" (He'll remember past successes, past failures, and important people in his life whom he has observed doing such things.)

If Hap's personal analysis turns out more "plus" than "minus," he'll let you know, "O.K., I'll do it!" You'll have yourself a real live volunteer...but how motivated is he, really?

Motivation takes energy. And even though Hap has said "Yes," you still don't know for sure what his motives are. Maybe he just wants to have his picture taken for the newspaper and when that's done, he'll be done! The amount of energy Hap turns on will be governed by the strength of his commitment, and commitment is related in some mysterious way to his values, interests, needs and self-concept.

Let's make some guesses about his motives...
• If his primary motive was his *value* of a beautiful environment, Hap is likely to volunteer for projects related to
improving the quality of life in the wilds, and he will probably
try to convert others to his beliefs while doing more than his
share of the work.
• If his primary motive was a *need* to know how to barbecue
fish, Hap may work hard building a pit, collecting wood,
cleaning fish so that he can learn from the number one fish
chef.
• If his primary motive was an *interest* in a particular person
who had also volunteered, Hap will probably work as long as
he can work alongside his potential friend.

This discussion of Hap's motivation is oversimplified and
somewhat contrived, of course, but the basic dynamics described are real and *do operate.* This brief description of what
turns Hap on will help you remember some of the essentials of
motivation as you work with the members of your own group.

To summarize: remember these two conditions when you
want to motivate others:
• Motivation is a process *within* the individual, and therefore,
the "motivat*ee*" is the one who is in total control of the situation, not the leader. Hap and his friends — the members of
your group — know and are in control of their unique individual ... values ... needs ... interests ... self-concepts.

What's more, only Hap can determine ... his chances of
success and his readiness to take risks ... what his motives
are when he says, "I'll do it" ... when he will "turn
on" .. how much energy he will give ... when he will "turn
down" or "turn off."
• The *motivator* (you) may have some luck with expanding
Hap's awareness of his options, helping him get in touch with
his interests, and creating opportunities for him in your
group. Anything beyond that is a very uncertain process of
making inferences about Hap's motivational self based on
what he says and does. Only through practice and spending
time with Hap, can you become better at knowing what he's
about. (And, of course, he is only one of your many members!)

Ten Ways to Increase Your Chances of Motivating Others

There are some fairly simple things you can do that will give you a head start on membership motivation. Read 'em and reap (the rewards):

1. Provide low-threat situations that make it easy for new or shy members to speak up, and *listen* to what they are saying.

2. Give members with limited experience and low self-confidence something relatively simple to do at first, or include them in a small-group effort with friendly and experienced models.

3. Look for non-verbal signals (facial expressions, eye contact, posture, tone of voice) that your members give you and be responsive to what you see. There is lots more going on non-verbally among people than words alone will tell you.

4. Use people's first names (make a habit of *remembering* them!), and mingle and talk with members as they work. Be generous with positive suggestions and compliments. Let them know you know they're there and tell them you missed them when they're absent. (A phone call to Hap the day after a missed meeting may let him feel ''noticed'' for the first time!)

5. Involve members in setting organizational goals, choosing projects, and discussing issues, using small groups whenever possible.

6. Divide projects and committee work into as many manageable parts as possible *before* asking for volunteers to do the work. Encourage people to seek new experiences rather than ask them to do the same thing over and over again. (Hap may be your most effective poster maker, but he'll burn out fast if that's all he ever gets to do for the group.)

7. Get a sense of what people are seeking from the organization by spending informal time with them individually and helping them find things to do that match their interests.

8. Involve members in the business of the organization itself, to strengthen their sense of ''ownership'' of the group.

9. Encourage cooperation and teamwork...reward positive interaction and mutual support among members as they work together.

10. Be informal and personable, and get your hands "dirty" once in a while without getting too deeply involved in details which might limit your perspective of "the big picture."

Participation and involvement represent the most direct line to a person's motivational "buttons." The idea of motivating or "turning on" another person directly is a myth. All you can do is to get to know your people, then manage the structure, atmosphere, and activities of the group in ways that will give each individual both the will and the opportunity to get involved.

For Further Reading

• Ackerman, Leonard, "Let's put motivation where it belongs... within the individual." *The Personnel Journal,* July, 1977.

One cannot motivate another; motivation comes from within and requires an atmosphere of openness, communication of needs, and flexibility.

• Hersey, Paul and Blanchard, Kenneth H., *Management of Organizational Behavior: Utilizing Human Resources.* Englewood Cliffs: NJ: Prentice-Hall, Inc., 1977, pp. 15-81.

Key leadership resources are described: motives, goals, motivational strength, situation, expectancy and availability, needs and motivational environment.

• Herzberg, Frederick, "Motivation-hygiene profiles: Pinpointing what ails the organization." *Organization Dynamics,* Autumn, 1974.

A diagnostic approach to determining the state of health of an organization. Running a fever? Showing signs of tension and pressure? Going into shock? Six profiles describe the most common attitude problems found in organizations.

• McDonald, Frederick J., *Educational Psychology.* San Francisco: Wadsworth Publishing Co., Inc., 1959.

Motivation defined in terms of energy change, need satisfaction, incentives, attitudes, values and goals.

3

Communicating
Ideas and Feelings

What Is Your Communication Style?

Are you a *one-way communicator?* Do you believe that (1) an elected leader is supposed to *LEAD*; (2) all others are meant to *FOLLOW*; and (3) being an articulate, persuasive speaker-parliamentarian is the most effective way to motivate members?

> One-way communicators seem to view the human head as a jug...and that members are "jugheads" whose only real value is to soakup words well chosen by their leaders.

Or are you a *two-way communicator* who believes that the election of a leader represents an unwritten mandate (1) to involve the membership in all major decisions; (2) to bring out the potential in every member; and (3) to achieve understanding among all members through *active listening* and the hearty reception of all helpful forms of feedback and questioning?

> Two-way communicators believe that people come to understand each other by combining *all* of what is said, heard, and seen; the more open the interaction ...the greater the degree of understanding.

If you'd rather be identified with the "two-way folks," don't stop now, for the rest of this chapter describes ways to make this two-way communication process an important and valuable part of your style of leadership.

The Four Components of Interpersonal Communication

When two people attempt to communicate an idea or a feeling, four components influence the process and the results: (1) the entry, (2) the message sent, (3) the message received, and (4) the personal interaction. Let's take a closer look at each, and how three of the four can be "shaped up" to produce better communication.

THE ENTRY

Each person enters the communication with a unique package of personal attributes and dispositions: deeply-held values, needs, interests, self-concepts, and special perspectives. The more different the packages, the less likely it is that the spoken message of one will convey an identical meaning to the other. Every communication attempt

Zelda   Abner

Two unique "packages" of values, needs, interests, self-concepts, and perspectives.

between you and another will be "tilted" to some degree by this disparity. There is little which can be done about this component which exists at the outset.

THE MESSAGE SENT

The message itself is meant to transfer meaning to another person. How it is worded and how it is delivered makes all the difference in the way it is received by others. Here are nine ways to help insure that your audience (one person or many) understands the meaning you intended for them to hear in the first place:

YOUR PLACE, OR MINE?

Zelda's unique organic computer selects words and style and induces her body to function accordingly.

1. Know *why* you want to speak. What outcomes do you seek ... understanding ... cooperation ... agreement ... approval ... acceptance?

2. Make it brief. *Everything* you say and do should contribute to your desired outcome. Say and do no more than that!

3. Know *what* you want to say before you start talking. Rambling, repetition, or long pauses will cause your audience to wander into worlds of their own...or take up doodling.

4. Use words and phrases your audience will understand.

5. Use motivational language that relates to their current needs and interests. Talk about: opportunity ... recognition belonging ... satisfaction ... love.

6. Avoid using "I" excessively; they'll get tired of hearing "I need," "I want," "I know," "I believe," "I think," "I suggest," and "I don't."

7. Reinforce your words with body language; project your feelings with your eyes, your face, your hand and arm gestures, your posture, your *tone* of voice.

8. Involve your audience by asking them questions. Causing them to think turns them on and activates their brain cells.

9. Use "main-idea" words to help your audience organize their listening ... "Our goal is to ...." ... "To summarize this point ...." ... "Remember these two things ...."

THE MESSAGE RECEIVED

Messages received are altered
and, to a certain extent, determined by the disparity between
the unique systems of personal
experience of the persons involved. The greater the differences,
the more difficult it will be to
achieve understanding. The
meaning of a message can also
be lost in the listening process

Abner's unique organic
computer filters the words
and images received and
flashes "tilt" — or — "not
programmed for previous
command."

itself. *Most of us speak at about
150 words per minute, whereas
we can hear and comprehend at
the rate of about 500 words per
minute!!* That is one reason listeners' minds wander on all
sorts of excursions when the speaker's style is ineffective.

Let's consider some ways to use this "excess listening
time" in the interest of good communication:

1. Analyze what is being said and take notes if it will help
you retain the key points. (Caution: Don't get so absorbed in
note-taking that you lose concentration on the on-going
message.)

2. Get the gist of *WHY* the speaker's comments are important to you or the organization and make a note of it. (See Item
1 in "The Message Sent.")

3. Listen for main points.

4. Listen for facts offered to support each main point.

5. Summarize main points and supporting facts period-
ically. This will help you *retain* the substance of what is said
and may raise questions about those things that are *not* being
said.

6. Watch to see what feelings are being communicated by
the speaker: Are there non-verbal signals, voice inflections,
gestures, finger-tapping, eye movements, a change in the
brow, even silence that give you clues about the real
message? Communication is a lot more than words alone.

THE PERSONAL INTERACTION

Understanding does not result just from sending and receiving messages, no matter how effective these components of communication are. Both the sender and the receiver have needs that require additional verbal interaction. The sender needs to know...was my message clear? Was my objective achieved? Were my facts absorbed? Does the listener *really* understand? The receiver has needs to answer back, and ask questions about the meaning of the statement.

When the speaker has spoken and the listener has listened, two-way communication takes "center stage." Questions, suggestions, new insights, new ideas, and new understandings.

When two-way communication is flowing openly, listeners hear and understand the sender's messages, and offer "feedback," often expressing new ideas which result in a richer outcome than the speaker initially intended.

Here are some examples of helpful interaction:
• "Are you saying that you believe we should have an audit of our books done at the end of each year?" (paraphrasing)
• "Your committee has given us an excellent recommendation, but could you tell us what other alternatives you have considered, and why the one you have selected is the best?" (requesting more information)
• "What did you mean when you said ....?" (clarifying)
• "I'm having trouble agreeing with you because ....; can you help me?" (resolving differences)
• "I didn't hear everything you just said; would you say it again, please?" (repeating)

Asking Questions

Personal interaction questions are crucial to effective two-way communication: they open people up, get them involved, and develop understanding.

Six key question words are WHO? ... WHAT? ... WHEN? WHERE? ... WHY? ... HOW?

WHO can help us with this?
WHAT would change their minds?
WHEN do we begin?
WHERE is the information we're missing?
WHY do you want to do it that way?
HOW will we get support?

Avoid these five question words, which may get you nothing but one-word answers: DO...? IS...? WILL...? CAN...? ARE...?

In summary, communicating ideas and feelings openly while taking into account the other person's perceptual world is the essence of a healthy organization. Effective communication is a *must* if you hope to develop understanding of ideas, make the best possible decisions, and involve a variety of individual members in the activities of the organization.

For Further Reading

- Banet, Anthony G., "Thinking and feeling." *AHGF, 1973,* pp. 139-141.

  Both *thinking* and *feeling* are essential to constructive communication. *Thinking* leads to a rational explanation of the interaction, and *feeling* leads to a deeper understanding of it.

- Cinnamon, Kenneth M. and Matulef, Norman J., *Human Relations Development* (Volume 3). Kansas City, MO: C.M.A. Publication Co., 1979, pp. 11-24.

  Interpersonal communication is *basic* to human relations development. Presents a six stage/five level model (from saying "Hello" to expressing feelings). Eight communication skills with examples (listening, problem solving, confrontation, feedback, self-disclosure, interviewing, self-expression, assertiveness).

- Combs, Gary W., "Defensive and supportive communications." *AHGF, 1981,* pp. 113-116.

  Analysis of two communication styles: one, motivated by the need to control, uses persuasion to convince the listener; the other, based upon interaction, grasps both fact and feeling of what others say through clarifying and checking.

- Gibb, J.R., Platts, Grace N. and Miller, Lorraine F., *Dynamics of Participative Groups.* St. Louis, MO: John S. Swift Co., Inc., 1951, pp. 29-30.

  Overview of effective communication, with examples of adequate and poor styles.

- Luthi, J. Ryck, "Communicating communications." *AHGF, 1978,* pp. 123-127.

  Analysis of factors affecting the sender (self-feelings, belief in assertive rights, perception of the message, and feelings about the receiver); suggestions for effective expression; points for the listener; responses that block effective communication; awareness of feelings.

- Morris, Kenneth T. and Cinnamon, Kenneth M., *A Handbook of Verbal Group Exercises.* Kansas City, MO: Applied Skills Press, 1974 and 1975 editions.

  300 pages of goal-oriented group exercises: assessment, awareness, communication, feedback, feelings, listening, roles, self-concept, and more.

- Nichols, Ralph G., *Effective Listening.* Rochester, NY: Xerox Corporation, 1964.

  Four tape recordings describe important aspects of listening, its effect upon relationships, and how to improve listening and communication skills.

- Nichols, Ralph G., *Listening is a Ten-Part Skill.* Chicago: Enterprise Publications, 1952.

  Valuable resource on listening by much-quoted authority in the field of communications.

- Pfeiffer, J. William, "Conditions which hinder effective communications." *AHGF, 1973,* pp. 120-123.

  Briefly discussed are: preoccupation, emotional blocks, hostility, charisma, past experiences, hidden agendas, inarticulateness, stereotyping, physical environment, mind-wandering, defensiveness, relationships, and status.

- Wismer, Jack N., "Communication effectiveness: Active listening and sending feeling messages." *AHGF, 1978,* pp. 119-122.

4

Working With Cultural and Other Differences

The uniqueness of individual differences is a special challenge for leaders of volunteers. Extra measures of awareness, sensitivity, and flexibility are required to involve members of different *cultural backgrounds,* those who are much *older or younger* than most members, those who may have *physical disabilities,* and even those who are of a "minority" *sex* when they are far outnumbered in your group.

You will find in this chapter that emphasis is on ethnic and cultural differences. By and large, multicultural organizations are more common, and they are especially demanding because of the potential for misunderstanding, conflict, and member dropout. While we have chosen *culture* as our working example of important differences among members, we trust to your understanding and flexibility in adapting these ideas to the specific needs of your own situation.

If you have never worked with a group whose members come from a variety of backgrounds, you are missing one of the richest, most rewarding "happenings" life has to offer. At the same time, being the leader of a widely diverse group of people can be a bit unnerving at first. Don't let the challenge lead you to ignore or gloss-over the realities of the situation, however.

Whatever your role in your multi-cultural group, start by keeping a couple of things in mind:

• Most people of color have pretty much discarded the notion of the United States as a "melting-pot" of different races, cultures, and nationalities. They argue that this view of American society down-plays the importance of their heritage and works against the retention of customs, values and beliefs that they cherish. Cultural integration and equality of opportunity are worthy goals, but total assimilation into the majority culture is not; not, at least, if the intention is to strip away

the last vestiges of their heritage or rob them of their cultural identity. Sensitive and fair-minded leaders in a multi-cultural organization prefer to *accent* interpersonal equality and to *celebrate* diversity!
• Those who have not had formal power tend to be suspicious of those who do. American history now clearly shows that Blacks, Asians, Native Americans and Hispanics in this country were repeatedly used and abused by people of wealth, position or power by virtue of race alone. Similar feelings may exist for any group of people who come from a background of oppression or exploitation; use *your* power carefully.

We're going to assume you accept those basic points about cultural differences, and move on to some things you can *do* in your organization to increase interpersonal awareness and sensitivity to differences. (Note that all of the other getting-acquainted and group process suggestions contained in this book will work no matter *what* the composition of the group. Our consistent theme is that effective leaders are those who are aware of and able to respond to the varied needs and values of the members.)

Individual Steps for Improving Awareness of Differences

• Establish a better historical perspective of the differences represented in your organization. Take the initiative by reading, asking questions, getting involved in small group discussions, and showing a general commitment to learn and to understand.
• Develop a contemporary frame of reference about culture... read about current and emerging racial/cultural issues.
• Be sensitive to different forms of media. Watch for stereotypes and cliches. For example: the whole Black world is *not* related to the ''Jeffersons'' of TV fame....
• Check your facts before you form a cultural opinion or make a statement.
• Be sensitive to and knowledgeable about specific, contemporary cultural differences such as language, humor, and gestures.

- Read cultural magazines, newspapers and books; listen to cultural radio programs.
- Take some risks. Attend an event which is programmed by and for a group other than your own.
- Seek out introductory classes, workshops, or seminars on culture and/or race relations, handicaps, equality of the sexes.
- Don't be defensive...be open and listen.

Group Activities for Improving Awareness of Differences

- *Goals and objectives* which reflect and embrace the cultural diversity of your membership.
- Majority membership *workshops* on awareness of cultural differences.
- *Discussions of tokenism:* What is it? How is it used? Does it apply to your organization?
- *Cross-cultural exchanges* (pot-lucks, socials, entertainment, discussions, lectures, art exhibits,...)
- *Presentations* by prominent local leaders from different backgrounds on culture, racism, art, politics, equal opportunity,...
- Small *support groups* — "networks" — within the larger organization to help people feel secure and welcome.
- *Programs* which improve understanding of the values of people of different cultures, races, ages, physical abilities, sexes. (Follow up by *incorporating* those diverse values into the procedures and activities of the group.)
- *Support systems* which guarantee participation for those of different backgrounds.
- *Leadership and risk-taking* by the leader(s) to establish greater multicultural participation.
- *Meeting places and times* which allow the widest possible participation (e.g., is your meeting place accessible to the handicapped?).
- A "*buddy system*" which pairs majority and minority members to discuss differences and similarities in traditions, values, and life experiences.

These suggestions only begin to scratch the surface of activities and techniques which, if sincerely used, will move your organization toward being more culturally aware and responsive. Such a commitment should not be made by the titled leaders or executive officers alone, however. The effort will fail miserably if the entire membership does not support it. A great deal of leader "homework" may be needed here to prepare members to act positively, and to avoid awkward and potentially damaging reactions to diversity.

In order for many people of difference to be able to contribute their ideas, concerns, and creativity without fear, leaders must minimize procedural barriers in the organization. Ethnics are especially sensitive to the ways the majority culture has denied them access. This question is *not* one of ability, but of organizational sensitivity to language and cultural differences, access to group resources and decisions, enhanced self-confidence and feeling of belonging.

Take a close look at some of these common "roadblocks":

• *Parliamentary Procedure:* For many members from other cultures, formal parliamentary procedure may be a threat. Some might even view it as oppressive. Techniques must be established for developing a greater understanding of its value and how it can be used effectively to make decisions or to achieve goals.

• *Bureaucratic Processes:* As is true of parliamentary procedure, long and complicated procedures may prove barriers to involvement. Unfamiliar forms and rules may represent a cumbersome way to get things done. (Indeed, *everyone* benefits from streamlined procedures!)

• *Communication Skills:* Be sensitive to language and colloquial differences among the membership. Be sure you strive for clear and precise communications, whether verbal or written (see Chapter Three). Don't try to impress anyone with your vocabulary; go for understanding, instead.

• *Assertive Skills:* When your heritage differs from that of most other members, being assertive in an organization may be very difficult. Imagine yourself in the minority: How easy would it be for you to speak out on an issue, make a motion,

question a leader? The scene can be very intimidating.
Special programs for all members should be provided to
respond to this need.

The primary emphasis of this chapter has been to make a
strong pitch to majority leaders and members of ethnically-
diverse volunteer organizations about the importance of
awareness and sensitivity to cultural and other differences.
Culture is not static: it is constantly changing and adapting.
To lead others effectively, you must provide activities, events,
and programs for the entire membership which improve
awareness of and response to differences in culture, age, sex,
and physical abilities. The key is not to ignore the differences
among people, but to recognize diversity as a real source of
excitement, growth, and challenge. Celebrate!

We'd like to give credit to two people who gave us valuable
feedback and suggestions about this chapter from their
cultural perspective: Ms. Greer Wilson (Hampton Institution)
Ms. Delores Austin (University of California, Santa Barbara)

For Further Reading

- Alberti, Robert E. (Ed.), *Assertiveness: Innovations, Applications, Issues.* San Luis Obispo, CA: Impact Publishers, 1977.
  Part 3, *Assertiveness Across Cultures*

- Baker, Gwendolyn C., "Multicultural education: An approach
that will insure success." Bloomington, IL: Association of College
Unions International, *Convention Proceedings, 1981* (keynote address
  Defines multicultural education; stresses the importance of a
multicultural approach, putting multiculturism into practice in and
beyond the classroom. Ms. Baker's model offers three components:
acquisition of knowledge, *development* of knowledge, and *involveme*

- Cheek, D.K., *Assertive Black...Puzzled White.* San Luis Obispo,
CA: Impact Publishers, 1976.
  An analysis of the black experience in America and its implications for the concept of "assertiveness." Stresses assumptions
inherent in inter-racial exchanges.

- Terry, Robert W., *For Whites Only.* Grand Rapids, MI:
Eerdmans, Center for Social Change (Oakland, CA), 1970.
  Stresses need for a new social consciousness in the white culture
to deal with racism in America.

Part 2

"Getting Started"

The lasting results of group life are those that come from positive interactions among the members...these depend on:
- How members feel about themselves
- How well members know one another
- How much members identify with the organization

Leaders, who come from the membership, are given a temporary "credit card" *by* the membership, with the expectation that the leader will help all in the group to grow from their relationships with one another and to accomplish *goals* they could never achieve alone. The six chapters which make up this part of *Lead On* present ways for leaders to make the most of the human factor that exists in all volunteer organizations.

READ ON!

5
Building Your Leadership Team

If you have ever been a member of a team, you know the exhilaration of being part of a common effort. How good it feels to:
- plan a group program and make it succeed,
- have a unique role to play and do it well,
- be needed by another team member and come through,
- be helped to feel "O.K." by others — and help others feel "O.K." too!

It is especially satisfying when things go well, of course. When things fall apart, however, team feelings continue to be supportive and fulfilling because when you are really a team, you can discuss openly how to benefit from your failures and how to help each other become even better individually.

There may not be another experience quite like the spirit of teamwork. You know you can do so much better working with others than alone. You've learned to be dependent on others while sensing their dependence on you. What is more, you can enjoy it all and become a better person in the process! That's what teamwork is all about in recreational sports...and that's what it can be among the officers of your organization.

Start by looking at your officers as an *organizational team.* You'll notice that your "team" has a lot going for it already:
- A common cause
- Individual roles to play
- Dependence on one another
- Feedback from each other to get better at your own jobs
- The capacity to work through differences to become a stronger, better unit
- Sharing and growing from "the thrill of victory and the agony of defeat"
- Time together "between games" to become good friends.

So You Want to Build an Officer Team?

Let's assume you are convinced: a group of officers who go through a term of office with a team attitude will be more effective than officers who do not. When should you get started? There's no doubt about it. The best time is the day election results are announced. If that day has long passed, don't "hang it up," just get everybody together as soon as possible. Establishing a team part way into the year is better than not doing it at all!

To become a team requires a lot more than just desire, of course. It takes time and it takes commitment. You'll probably have to have a few special meetings and informal get-togethers, perhaps before and after organizational meetings and activities. And you'll need to try new things and help one another grow — *intentionally,* not just by chance. *Openness with one another* and *pro-active feedback* (i.e., offering both positive and critical comments without waiting to be asked) will be two key "modus operandi."

Your officer team can succeed only if each individual understands...

...the mission or purpose of the organization,

...how the organization operates (by-laws, standing rules, procedures, finances, meetings, committees, and established communication networks),

...how members can contribute to the success of organization affairs (officers' responsibilities, opportunities for involvement, projects already under way).

The springboard for team-like behavior is for everyone to become knowledgeable about the organization!

The next essential is to personalize the group's structure by clarifying the role each individual will be playing. Get to know one another on a personal, individual level, and learn about each others' experiences, skills, and resources. (See Chapter Seven, "Helping Folks Get Acquainted.") Share personal goals, within the organization and beyond...whatever will help develop an understanding of each team member's values, needs, interests, priorities, aspirations,...even concerns and fears.

Don't be surprised if there is impatience with this team-building process during these early stages. You may hear such "encouraging" comments as, "Forget this stuff. What are we going to do about the financial situation? We're nearly bankrupt!" or... "I think we should be talking about what we should be *doing,* not how we're *feeling*!" If this does occur, and it's very likely that it will, assure the members that you are leading up to tackling issues and goals and that these experiences will speed up those processes when you get there. Groups go through definite stages, and it is important to develop trust and cohesiveness as foundations for the work which lies ahead.

Once you have become acquainted and explored each others' roles, responsibilities, experiences, resources and skills, it is time to become familiar with the specific skills required of team members. Precisely what is expected of each individual?

Figure 5-1 is a suggested list of teamwork skills. This "Tracking Chart" is meant to be used by individual team members to record improvement throughout their term in office. Start with self-ratings. At a team work-session, take time to discuss each item so that everyone will agree on what each statement means. Then, from time to time during the year at special team get-togethers, take a look at each person's progress on each skill, and get helpful feedback from teammates. (*Proactive feedback* should be encouraged whenever an occasion presents itself — not just at team meetings.)

Two special ways to make your team building experience more effective are to (1) take the leadership team to a place away from it all to spend full-time on this important process, and (2) bring in a consultant-facilitator to make your time spent most effective. These team-building options are discussed in the sections which follow.

TRACKING TEAMWORK SKILLS

Place the date (e.g., 4-27) in the column that best represents your skill level as you see it. Take into account any feedback you've received from teammates.

	Novice	So-So	Intermediate	Good	I've Arrived!
1. I ask others what they mean whenever I'm not geting the full meaning of what they are trying to tell me.					
2. I explain my motives fully, and give reasons for my actions so that there will be no guesswork in my relationship with others.					
3. I separate how I **feel** about a situation from what I **think,** and I tell others about both so they will know exactly "where I'm coming from."					
4. I am so direct and straight in my talk that others get the full impact of my message without having to attach other meanings to it.					
5. I really listen when people talk to me. I show that I **am** listening by looking at them and doing nothing else while they are talking.					
6. I check my assumptions about what people mean or need by asking them to tell me, rather than assuming that I know.					

	Novice	So-So	Intermediate	Good	I've Arrived!
7A. I know the values, needs, interests, and talents of other team members.					
7B. I act to take them into account within the organization.					
8A. I see the "big picture" of organizational activities.					
8B. I am aware of what others are doing, and as I do my part, I offer others whatever help I can give them.					
9. I believe that decisions by consensus are superior to those made any other way, and I: a. delay advocating my ideas, after stating them as clearly as I can, until listening to the reactions of others.					
b. oppose voting or bargaining when discussion reaches a stalemate, while I look for and advocate the next most acceptable alternative.					
c. refuse to betray my beliefs simply to avoid conflict or to reach harmony and agreement.					
10. I insist on a "huddle" to talk things over whenever all is not well within the team.					

The Retreat Experience

What is a Retreat?   • It's a *place* away from it all, away from telephones, noise and distraction.
- It's a *group* of people with a common cause.
- It's a *change of pace* from regulation and routine so you can relax and recreate.
- It's an *experience* with a purpose in a new kind of freedom.
- It's *time* to reflect, to plan, to learn, to grow.

What is the Purpose?   Retreats are planned around a goal or purpose. (See Chapter Twelve, "Goal Setting.") Examples:
- To develop an effective team of newly-elected officers and other key leaders.
- To teach new members the mission, structure, and traditions of the organization and to get them to know the leadership team and one another.

Who Should Attend?   Match 'n mix in whatever way will achieve your goal:
- New officers (team building)
- New members (to enlighten them about the organization)
- Anybody (to develop leadership or plan an activity)
- Everybody (just for fun)

How to Make it Happen?   • Decide on the purpose, program content, presenters, length, and who should attend.
- Adopt a budget (cost per person and necessary expenses)
- Appoint a coordinator and committee workers.
- Visit possible sites and check on meeting room sizes and facilities, food service, recreation, and overnight accommodations, if required.
- Check transportation options and details.
- Receive the retreat committee report and negotiate any changes desired.
- Sign a facilities use contract.
- Make it happen.
- Evaluate.

More Ideas on Where to Go? • *Conferencing in California,*
by Dawn Ungrue and Laurel
Gillespie, Impact Publishers, 1979, has information on
selecting an *informal* site in California, and planning helps for
informal retreats anywhere. For more elaborate accommodations, check with the Chamber of Commerce in the area of
your choice.

So You Want to Hire a Consultant-Facilitator!

What Do Consultants   • Manage training sessions,
Really Do?   making it possible for all mem-
                           bers of the leadership group to par-
  ticipate on an equal basis.
• Diagnose what is going on and *not* going on within the
  group; intervene whenever appropriate to clarify what is
  holding back group development.
• Encourage openness and acceptance during differences
  and conflict.
• "Pace" the group according to the rate of team development.

What to Look for in a   • Education and training in group
Consultant-Facilitator   process theory and practice, such
                           as professional programs of Na-
  tional Training Laboratory (Bethel, ME), University Asso-
  ciates (La Jolla, CA); advanced degrees; job experience as a
  group facilitator.
• Experience in leadership development in volunteer organi-
  zations.
• Membership in relevant professional societies, such as the
  National O.D. Network, American Society for Training and
  Development, American Psychological Association, Association for Specialists in Group Work.
• Ask for references!

Where to Find One   • Local college or university. Ask for
                           the Dean or Vice Chancellor for
  Student Services, or the department of business, psychology, education, sociology, or personnel.

- Yellow pages. Look up Human Service Organizations, Mental Health Agencies, Social Services and Welfare Organizations, Psychologists (group specialization).
- Training institutions and societies mentioned above.

How to Make the   • Be prepared to describe clearly the
Arrangements   goals you want to achieve so they can
                        make informed judgments about whom
to recommend.
- Insist on a written contract to avoid misunderstandings about who pays for travel, meals, lodging, preparation of materials, audio-visual equipment needed, preliminary planning time, time on-site; when payment is made; other key "details."
- Insist on a face-to-face meeting for planning purposes, if at all possible; otherwise, develop details by telephone and arrange to have an adequate exchange of ideas and plans by mail, summarized in the contract.
- *Note:* Take care that the Consultant-Facilitator is not perceived by members of the group as *your* personal choice to "shape them up." This can only be done if all arrangements and contacts are agreed to by the group, itself.

For More Information

More hints about hiring and working with consultants are offered in "Contracting: A process and a tool," by Francis L. Ulshak, La Jolla, CA: University Associates, *Annual Handbook for Group Facilitators, 1978,* pp. 138-142.

For Further Reading

- Francis, Dave and Young, Don, *Improving Work Groups: A Practical Manual for Team Building.* San Diego, CA: University Associates, 1979.
  Excellent sections on team-building process, team-review questionnaires, generating team development, and 46 activities for building strengths and clearing blockages. Written for management, but many applications to volunteer organizations.

• Hanson, Philip G., "Giving feedback: An interpersonal skill." *AHGF, 1975,* pp. 147-154.
Defines origin and meaning of "feedback" and describes the dynamics of giving and receiving feedback.

• Karp, H.B., "A Gestalt approach to collaboration in organizations." *AHGF, 1976,* pp. 203-210.

• Lau, James B., *Behavior in Organizations: An Experiential Approach.* Homewood, IL: Richard D. Irwin, Inc., 1975, pp. 193-200.
Excellent presentation of the development of team building, problems encountered, goals of team building, and how to plan and conduct a team-building workshop.

• Nylen, Donald et al., "Role functions in a group." *AHGF, 1976,* pp. 136-138.
Useful listing and description of task-related, group building and maintenance-related role functions required in groups. Nonfunctional group behavior is also identified.

• Pareek, Udal, "Developing collaboration in organizations." *AHGF, 1981,* pp. 136-138.
Excellent and thorough presentation of functional and dysfunctional forms of cooperation and competition, along with eight methods of intervention to build collaboration in organizations.

• Pfeiffer, J. William and Jones, John E., *A Handbook of Structured Experiences for Human Relations Training* (seven volumes as of 1982). San Diego, CA: University Associates.
Three team-building exercises are especially recommended: "Broken squares: Non-verbal problem solving" (Vol. 1, No. 7, pp. 25-30); "Team building: A feedback experience" (Vol. 3, No. 66, pp. 73-77); "Agenda setting, a team-building starter" (Vol. 5, No. 166, pp. 108-110).

• Reilly, Anthony J. and Jones, John E., "Team building." *AHGF, 1974,* pp. 227-237.
Excellent presentation of team-building in depth: what it is, its goals, how it is different, how to assume that it is done well. Specifics about conducting team-building sessions.

• Zander, A., "Team spirit vs. the individual achiever." *Psychology Today,* November, 1974.
A comparison of teamwork and individualism by an outstanding authority in group dynamics.

6

Leading Your First Meeting

The first activity that directly affects the membership is the first meeting of the year. A dynamite first meeting makes a winning first impression on members and creates optimistic expectations for the term ahead.

You'll find in this chapter an extensive plan for such a first meeting. We have in mind a group that has not met for several weeks, and is expecting a large number of potential new members to arrive as the new membership year begins. Such meetings often occur after summer vacation periods. We have witnessed one such meeting when more than 300 people showed up, without much warning! Unfortunately, the officers were unprepared, and the results were chaotic. A "What-the-Sam-Hill-happened?" discussion with the officers the following day helped us to develop the ideas that follow.

Let's begin with six absolute *Don'ts*:

1. Don't talk too much (remember *apathy*?)
2. Don't start late: it sets a pattern.
3. Don't feature any kind of outside program (not *this* meeting!)
4. Don't ask for volunteers! (There's a better way — see Chapter 13)
5. Don't call on anyone for a "report" if it can wait until a later meeting.
6. Don't read the minutes of the last meeting; it was many weeks ago, and *nobody cares!* (Anybody who really *does* can read them later!)

Next, we suggest your leadership team read through the next few pages, consider these ideas, select those that seem to fit your needs, then create a definite plan for your own first meeting.

Before the Meeting Starts

1. Have a "team plan"...make sure that everyone knows the total plan and is prepared for his/her part in it.
2. Make sure the meeting place can be easily identified from the outside, that it is well-lighted for a night meeting. Put up signs to get people to the room and a sign at the entrance, visible when the door is open or closed, that says something friendly, such as "Welcome New Members!"
3. Make sure that all meeting announcements and posters say clearly: "We start on time and adjourn early!" (Later on, prove it!)
4. Be sure that the agenda is ready beforehand, have copies for everyone, or be ready to project it on a screen, write it on newsprint, or otherwise post it for all to see.
5. See that the seating encourages maximum interaction among members and guests, that everyone can see the podium and hear what's going on, and that extra chairs are easily accessible. If you can, set up the room so that late-comers will enter at the rear, minimizing interruptions once you are under way.
6. Bring name tags and several marking pens.
7. Make certain that membership cards, change, receipts, and pens are ready.
8. Bring Membership Information Cards and a quantity of pens and pencils (sample form at the end of Chapter 7).
9. Prepare a display of club mementos...photos, your scrapbook, awards, newsletters, brochures, etc.
10. Prepare and bring enough copies of a printed handout about the organization for every person. Include a statement of the group's mission/purposes, a list of the officers and how to contact them, a list of opportunities for future involvement and whom to contact about each one, and a summary of recent organizational achievements.
11. Check to make sure the microphone is ready for use.

As People Enter the Room

Remember...you don't want their first impression of the organization to be their last!

12. Have old members come early and greet newcomers as they arrive, help them make out nametags, and talk with them individually or in groups of two to three. The "veterans" can also help with the other pre-meeting suggestions below.

13. Give everyone a Membership Information Card. Ask them to fill it out, then collect them immediately.

14. Give everyone the printed handout about the organization (Step 10), and invite them to look it over before the meeting starts.

15. Give everyone a copy of the meeting agenda and/or program, explaining those items which require further information.

16. Take everyone on a tour of whatever displays you have, or at least invite them to look them over.

17. Invite each person to join, in a friendly, non-pushy way. If they're interested, take them to the membership table; follow up after the meeting with those not yet ready to join.

Starting the Meeting

18. Ask team members and all other veterans present to help get everyone settled. Announce that it's time to get under way. At this point it's helpful to move membership and handout tables just outside the door to greet and sign up latecomers before they enter. In the meantime, the meeting can get started, rewarding those who arrived on time.

19. Introduce yourself. Personalize it and give people some information about who you are. Something like this: "Hi, everybody. Welcome to the Club Club! My name is Charlie Brown, and I'm your president for the coming year. I work at the supermarket down the street and go to school part-time at the community college. My wife, Susan, and our two children are here tonight, and I'd like you to meet them, too."

20. Welcome all new people attending and give them individual recognition, if at all possible. If time allows, let them introduce themselves: "It's good to see so many new faces here tonight. Will all the people who are here for the first time please stand? Thanks! Now, let's start over here to my left, and have each of you tell us a little bit about yourself." For large organizations, this is best done in small groups or by other methods described in Chapter 7. Also, in some situations, individuals attending for the first time may prefer not to be so "publicly" recognized. Use sensitivity here.
21. Welcome all returning members, and give them individual recognition similar to that afforded newcomers.
22. Acknowledge continuing members who have achieved special recognition (e.g.: community leaders, scholarship recipients, class or school officers).

Presenting Your Organization

23. Allow each officer to participate in the meeting in some major way. This helps out the president, gives them recognition, and lets others know who they are.
24. Explain the purpose of the organization, referring to the preprinted handout you gave to each attendee.
25. Explain the organization's committee structure — *briefly!* If it's the *least bit* complex, visual aids will be a big help, but keep it short and simple.
26. Highlight major past accomplishments and refer to the displays.
27. Review those continuing projects that will require involvement of the membership in the coming year.
28. Describe important upcoming events and emphasize how members and newcomers can get involved.
29. Explain important decisions the group may face during the year.
30. Announce committee appointments or name the appointments that will be made. Tell members how they can get on a committee.

31. Encourage members to come up with new program ideas (speakers, films, fund-raisers). Pass out cards on which they can jot down ideas; collect them at the end of the meeting.
32. Just for fun, have an auction, a drawing, a simple contest, or play a get-acquainted game. "Before we have refreshments, let's form a big circle in the middle of the room. Your position in the circle will be determined by the first letter in your first name...alphabetically, with the "A's" up here in this corner and the "Z's" over there." (See Chapter 7.)
33. Show slides or movies of past activities of the group.
34. Have refreshments.
35. End the meeting by introducing the key members again and asking them to go to designated areas of the room when you adjourn, to be accessible to interested persons.
36. Invite everyone to visit with the key members, and to turn in their "idea" and "Membership Information" cards.
37. Announce the next meeting — date, time, place, any items of business and the program.
38. End the meeting *on time* and at a high point of interest, not when members are exhausted and impatient.

After Adjournment

39. Make it easy for folks to locate individual leadership team members to chat with or to volunteer for various projects or committees.
40. Have old members seek out first timers who were not quite ready to join at the beginning of the meeting. Encourage veterans to ask newcomers if they have any questions, but *not to oversell!*
41. Have the "put-it-back-together" team clean up and put things away.
42. After it's all over, be sure the secretary writes up the minutes and the treasurer deposits the money!
43. The membership chair should begin to set up the Membership Information Card file to help various committee chairpersons identify and recruit new committee members.
44. The leadership team should evaluate the meeting, share individual feedback, and make plans for the next meeting.

The meeting we've just described may seem a little "heavy" compared to anything you've ever experienced. It is, but if your team puts together the right combination at the outset, you have a good chance of a successful season ahead. Such a carefully prepared meeting gets a lot of people acquainted, involved, and on their way home early. And — most important — they'll probably be back *next* meeting!

You probably will not want to do *everything* suggested above; few groups do! Your leadership team's jobs are to select the *important* things, and to do them *well.*

7

Helping Folks Get Acquainted

All of us have experienced attending a meeting of an organization for the first time. Everybody who's there is a stran-
ger and you find yourself alone in a crowd. No one comes up
to say "Hello." No one smiles or offers a hearty handshake.
So, you sit down in the nearest chair (the closer to the door,
the better), look around, and listen. When the meeting is
over, others leave in small groups, talking and laughing. You
(sob!) get up and leave in your own private capsule of empti-
ness, and stumble through the dark, lonely streets, still
searching for fulfillment (sigh)...

For some, this may be the first, last and only attempt to
break into that organization. Others may try again and again,
dropping hints of interest and intent, attending regularly,
paying dues, taking the initiative (and the risk) to meet new
people, tagging along with members of one clique or another.

Why are so many turned away by the organizational cold
shoulder when it's so easy and so human to make them feel
welcome and to help them get acquainted? When groups
make accessibility a priority, no one loses...it's a two-way,
everybody-wins situation.

In this chapter we'll look at some easy, non-threatening and
effective ways to help folks get acquainted. These activities
can help warm the atmosphere and prevent some of the damage done by "snap" first impressions. The goal is to help
people interact with one another from the start with a
minimum of bias, and a maximum of friendliness.

Situation I: A Newcomer Enters a Small Group:

• Stop what's going on, if you can, get a chair, enlarge the circle, walk toward the newcomer, *smile,* and reach out with a handshake, or a light touch to the arm or shoulder.
• Introduce yourself first, then find out what this new person likes to be called. (Matilda?) Introduce Matilda to others, or ask people to introduce themselves to her. Then briefly inform her what you're discussing and invite her to join right in.
• Before the discussion is over, be sure Matilda hears her own voice. Ask for her opinion, ideas, and questions.
• Before she leaves, tell Matilda when the next meeting will be, give her information and materials about the group, ask her if she'd like to receive your newsletter. Get her name, address, and telephone number, but don't push *formal* affiliation: membership or dues yet. (Save the "hard sell" at *least* until her second meeting...)

Situation II: Newcomers Enter a Large Group:

• Be prepared. Make one or more of your officers or continuing members responsible for welcoming first timers. Station this "newcomer team" at the entrance to the room, with helpers as needed to greet new people, the physically impaired, or others who may need assistance or information.
• Consider a one-to-one arrangement: one continuing member to one newcomer to get acquainted, introduce others before the meeting starts, sit together, ask about receiving the newsletter, and get name, address, and telephone number for follow-up contacts.
• Arrangements should be made to continue such contact with these newcomers at the following meeting, so that they can meet other members and begin to consider the more formal membership processes.
• All these steps should continue meeting after meeting with this special "newcomer team" quietly carrying out their welcoming function and keeping in touch with their increasing flock of new members.

• If your group is large enough — say 20 or more at a meeting — that a newcomer could go unnoticed, make it a regular agenda item to *ask* if there are new people present. Then arrange for your newcomer team to go into action and make contact with them.

Situation III: The First Meeting of a Newly-Formed Group or Committee of 5 to 15 Members:

A. *Who Am I?* (A structured interview and introduction by another person)
• Ask each member to pair up with another member, preferably someone they don't know at all. This can be done haphazardly, or you can ask them to count off, A-B-A-B...
• Give each person some paper and a pencil. Five- by 8-inch cards are ideal; be prepared to supply them.
• Ask the A's to interview the B's for five minutes, then have the B's repeat the process with the A's, using questions prepared for them in advance. You might include such items as...
   ...name, nickname, family, job, schools, travel, interests
   ...why they are interested in this group's work or goal
   ...what they hope to get from taking part
   ...how they can help most with the committee's job
   ...what they like most about meetings
   ...what they like least about meetings.
• When the ten minutes of interviews are up, rearrange everyone into a circle and give each person two minutes to introduce her or his partner to the group. (You may want to extend an invitation to others to ask additional questions of the person being introduced...although this takes a little more time, it does tend to "warm up" the atmosphere of this process.)
• The person in charge of this activity should be involved too, either as a member of a pair or by making a self-introduction.
• Name tags (on clothing) or name plates (on tables) can be added to help people call each other by name. Be certain they are printed large enough for all to see.

B. *WHO AM I?* (A structured self-introduction)
• Each person needs paper and pencil. Five- by 8-inch cards (again) are ideal...be prepared to supply them.
• Encourage everyone to participate fully, and do so yourself.
• Use instructions such as these (edit the questions as needed to "fit" your situation): "This get-acquainted activity will give everyone an opportunity to introduce him/herself to the group. I'll be asking questions for you to answer very briefly on your card. Just take notes for your own use on each question. The card is yours and will not be turned in. Do you have any questions? Okay, here we go...

Question 1: 'What's your name (or nickname if you prefer)?'
Question 2: 'What's the name of the place where you spent the happiest three consecutive days of your life?'
Question 3: 'Where do you go when you want to be alone... where's your special place to think or dream?'
Question 4: 'Who is *the* person in your life who brings you happiness and joy...makes you smile when you see him/her?'
Question 5: 'Who is someone you *really* respect and admire (living or dead; fictitious or real; met or unmet — *not family*)?'
Question 6: 'During what calendar year did you experience the most significant personal growth?'
Question 7: 'Name three to six things about yourself you're proud of...things you can do well, that make you feel kind of special.' "

• Repeat the questions, if necessary. Give people a few minutes to think about their answers and to write them down.
• Give each person a turn introducing him/herself from the notes they've taken, leaving out the answers to any question(s) they wish.

Situation IV: The First Meeting of a Very Large Group:

A. *WHO AM I?* (A structured self-introduction)
• Organize everyone into groups of five to ten people and ask them to sit in small circles. (See Chapter 15, "Leading Informal Discussions.)
• Select either of the alternative activities just described in Situation III.

B. *WHO ARE YOU?* ("Mingle Bingo")
• Place the name of every participant on a scrap of paper and put them in a fish bowl, a hat or a box (for a later drawing).
• Give everyone a heavy-stock card (8½ by 11 inches or larger) prepared in advance with squares containing descriptive phrases: red hair, left-handed, brother in military, wears contact lenses, expert windsurfer, shoe size 10-B, no cavities, on the executive committee, etc. Be creative and, if possible, try to match each statement to at least one person present.
• Invite everyone to mingle and ask everyone else, "Are you left-handed?" etc. When a person says "Yes" to a question, the name should be printed in the appropriate square.
• When several people have their cards completely filled out (i.e., when at least half the group has a name in every square), begin drawing the members' names out of the bowl, box or hat, one at a time. When a name is drawn, people should put an "X" in the square on their card where that name appears.
• As soon as someone has a horizontal, diagonal, or vertical "run" of the names drawn, it's "BINGO!" and the game is over. If you have the time, it's fun to find out who wrote which names in what squares...some folks will really surprise you!

NOTE: People who win tend to get a little "nasty" if they don't win a prize, so you might want to pick up a little something...)

C. *LIVING NAME TAG MINGLE*

• Give everyone a large card (about 10 by 12 inches) with a hole in each corner, tied with a string long enough to reach over the head and around the neck. Each person will also need to have a dark-colored crayon or felt pen.

• Give the group these instructions: "Print the following in large letters, about ¾ inch high, leaving space for seven lines:

1. Your first name.
2. The year you joined this club, or "new," or "visitor."
3. Your favorite leisure activity.
4. Name of the last book you read or are now reading.
5. Name of last movie you saw (or favorite movie).
6. Languages you speak.
7. The thing you can do really *well* and makes you *proud.*"

• Ask everyone to put the strings over their heads and mingle slowly (while music is playing and *without* speaking at all) so that others can see their answers.

• After several minutes (time depends on size of your group), ask each individual to pick another person he or she would like to get to know, then to sit down with that person and get acquainted. (Stop the music while people talk and get to know each other.)

• After about five minutes, ask the groups of two to mingle around the room (music playing, no talking) and look for another group of two they would like to get to know. Stop the music after about five minutes, and ask the groups of four to sit down and get acquainted.

• Repeat one more time to form groups of eight.

• Be certain that no individual, group of two, or group of four is left "out in the cold" when each of the above steps is completed. Encourage them to merge into a group even though it's not exactly two, four, or eight in size!

• Since groups of eight are excellent for small-group discussions, and because this is an excellent opportunity for members to get to know one another beyond the "name, rank and serial number" level, you may want to give them a specific topic to discuss for 15 to 20 minutes...

...What do you hope to get out of membership in this club?

...What skills, leadership experience, useful equipment, "connections," can you contribute to the club's activities?

The ideas we've given you in this chapter to help folks get acquainted are just a few of the many options available. As you can see, each can easily be changed to fit your own group's personality. Use your imagination in devising an on-going system to help every person enjoy the warm feelings that come from being recognized, being mentioned *by name,* and knowing what it means to *belong.* Your group will be a highly attractive one to join!

For Further Reading

• Forbess-Greene, Sue, *The Encyclopedia of Icebreakers.* St. Louis, MO: Applied Skills Press, 1980.

150 structured activities that warm-up, motivate, challenge, acquaint, and energize.

• Morris, Kenneth T. and Cinnamon, Kenneth M., *A Handbook of Verbal Exercises.* Kansas City, MO: Applied Skills Press, 1979.

341 pages of structured exercises, including getting acquainted and icebreakers.

• Pfeiffer, J. William and Jones, John E., *Annual Handbook for Group Facilitators* (annually since 1972) and *Handbook of Structured Experiences for Human Relations Training* (eight volumes since 1969). La Jolla, CA: University Associates.

A wealth of structured exercises (328 as of 1982) sometimes referred to as the "folk music" of human relations. Some formal, others informal, all have a purpose. Getting acquainted, forming subgroups, building trust, building openness, and many other categories.

• Weinstein, Matt and Goodman, Joel, *Playfair: Everybody's Guide to Noncompetitive Play.* San Luis Obispo, CA: Impact Publishers, 1980.

Sixty indoor and outdoor games...just for fun.

8

Finding Members' Interests

The better you know me and I know you, the better the chance that we'll become good friends and co-workers. What to say after "Hello" is no problem when you know something ...almost anything...about the other person's interests. As noted in the chapter on motivation, a person's interests are the most visible part of his/her "inner self"...more "public" by far than values or needs.

The previous chapter, "Helping Folks Get Acquainted," will help groups of strangers break down the icy awkwardness of not knowing others who are present at a meeting or activity. In this chapter we look at the membership as a whole and help answer the question, "How do you find out what interests individual members have?" Your leadership team needs this information to better involve members in the work and play of the organization.

Here are some ways to learn members' interests:
• Ask for volunteers to do a certain job — then pay attention to who actually shows up. (This doesn't mean that those who show are ultimately interested in just that particular job, however. Their *real* interest may be getting involved in *anything,* or in meeting other volunteers!)
• Interview new members by telephone and ask them direct questions about opportunities for their involvement and their related interests. This should be done for *all* new members on a general basis, rather than "calling around" for volunteers for a particular task at the last minute.
• Hold small-group sessions of new members with a leadership team member, perhaps during a portion of a larger group meeting. Stimulate informal talk about interests — and ask someone to take notes!
• At the first meeting of the year, place signs around the room, indicating primary areas of your organization's activities. Take a "working recess" to give everyone a chance to go to the area(s) of their main interests, talk to designated members of the leadership team, receive special materials, and sign up.
• Have every member complete a *Membership Information Card* to indicate their interests and other information valuable to the organization. This card should be tailored to fit your organization. It might be helpful, for example, to be able to locate a photographer, someone who has a bus-driver's license, a pick-up truck, or access to a special place for an informal meeting. Use a 4 x 6 inch or a 5 x 8 inch index card file, or an 8½ x 11 inch binder.

An information card should be completed whenever a new person joins your group. Keep them up to date, and use them for selecting members for committee work, special assignments, and nomination to leadership posts. The cards can also be very useful for computerizing membership information and for producing up-to-date mailing lists.

The next chapter, "Helping 'First Timers' Become Active Members," will lean heavily on such a systematized membership record.

MEMBERSHIP INFORMATION CARD

Last Name   **First Name**

Address

Telephone

INTERESTS:

(Check ☐ level of interest in each item; add others if you like)	High	Some	Little
Learning Leadership Skills	☐	☐	☐
Learning to do new things	☐	☐	☐
Getting to know others	☐	☐	☐
Public speaking	☐	☐	☐
Group discussions	☐	☐	☐
Keeping records	☐	☐	☐
Writing	☐	☐	☐
Community service	☐	☐	☐
Improving the environment	☐	☐	☐
Political activities	☐	☐	☐
Organizing events	☐	☐	☐
Publicity	☐	☐	☐
Social activities	☐	☐	☐
Recreation...outdoor	☐	☐	☐
Recreation...indoor	☐	☐	☐
Fund-raising	☐	☐	☐

EXPERIENCE...SKILLS... RESOURCES (Anything to help)

PERSONAL GOALS: (What would you like to achieve
as a member of this organization?)

9
Changing "First Timers" Into Active Members

"Hooking" a person into active membership after that first nibble at the organization is, like motivation, largely controlled within that individual. It is not within your power to make it stick by providing hefty incentives or laying on lots of persuasion. We can *assume* that people are attracted to a meeting of the Ski Club because they like to ski, or need a line on where to buy or rent equipment, or want to learn how to ski. In reality, these people may be visiting all sorts of clubs to get an overall view of the options available. They may just be looking for a group of people they would be comfortable with — regardless of its purpose.

If the act of attending a meeting is not enough, one sure way to get a better understanding of first-timers' level of interest is to *ask* them. A simple form like this may help:

Dear Potential Member:

Please let us know how we can best serve your particular interest in the goals and activities of the *Citizens for Greener Grass on This Side of the Mountain.* Check the appropriate items on this card and mail it to the president of CGGTSM. (It is already addressed and stamped.)

☐ I am interested in your goals, please send more information.
☐ Just send me your newsletters for now.
☐ I am interested in your organization and will attend meetings, but I'm not ready to join just yet.
☐ I am interested in your organization and want to join.
☐ I need transportation to the meetings.
☐ Other:

Name
Address
Telephone

Not learning the *real* needs and interests of potential new members can lead the group to "turn them off" by all sorts of inappropriate recruiting tactics.

Let's assume that Fred finally signs up. He's paid his dues, is a card-carrying "joiner," attends meetings, and is classified in the by-laws as a "regular" member. Is Fred an *active member?* How can you tell when a person is an *active member?* Try this checklist:

☐ Does s/he understand the purpose of the organization and express it clearly to others?

☐ Is s/he familiar with goals and traditions and does s/he explain them clearly to others?

☐ Does s/he call other members by their first names and do others do the same to him/her?

☐ Does s/he volunteer for a fair share of committee work and projects?

☐ Does s/he participate in meetings through discussion and voting?

If these are the criteria of active membership, how does Fred graduate from being a "joiner" to being an "active"? Whose responsibility is it to get him there, his or the group's? The best policy for an organization that is concerned about developing "joiners" into "actives" is to take the initiative. If you leave it entirely up to the "joiner," both may be disappointed!

Here are some things you can do:

• Set up some small group discussions for new members about the purpose of the organization. Include a charismatic "old timer" in the group to guide this orientation experience with important facts. Give them some printed materials to keep.

• Do the same for long-term goals and traditions.

• Take steps to be certain that new members get to know a significant number of *active* members by name. Fred will become known to them in the process. Give him a list of members, with addresses and telephone numbers, for his personal use.

• Become aware of his primary interests (review Chapter 8) and make it easy for him to get involved in these kinds of activities.

• Arrange frequent, small-group informal discussions for the organization. Fred will get caught up in the low-key, personalized atmosphere and express his ideas and feelings more easily.

• Contact him when he misses a meeting or activity and say "We really missed having you there!"

• Have an active member informally "keep in touch" when he seems to be "on his own," especially if Fred is a little tentative about getting involved.

• Try an all-day or weekend retreat with special programming for new members. The informal, relaxed, fun-oriented atmosphere may help reinforce the things you can only talk about during meetings and small-group discussions.

Helping "first-timers" become active members should be seen as the organization's responsibility. While it is true that some new members will become active on their own, it is in everyone's best interest for the organization to take the lead.

10

Informing the Members

Every member wants to know what's happening. If they all lived near each other and attended all the meetings and activities, the task of keeping everyone informed would be simple; perhaps a bulletin board centrally located would be sufficient. But members and officers are often widely scattered, with few opportunities to meet or to share experiences. Telephones, postcards, letters from the Chair, and newsletters can all help bridge the gap.

TELEPHONES are useful for touching base one-to-one or even for conferences of three or more. Pick a time when rates are cheap, and talk from an agenda and notes to be time-effective. (The telephone directory tells how to set up a conference call.) If possible, send the other party(ies) an agenda from your perspective; the other(s) can make additions before and during the call. In conference calling, someone must be in charge of "airtime"...to ask for opinions, questions, and facts from individuals by name, and to move the discussion along from item to item and point to point. Ask for closing agreement with..."Does anyone know of any reason this won't work?" or "Have we forgotten anything?...anybody?" Consider having the calls taped, or designate someone to take notes and distribute them promptly.

A "telephone chain" can also be an effective way to get information out and/or to get feedback from the membership. Select a group of reliable volunteers and divide the membership into lists of five or ten...the volunteers will not be overburdened and information will flow quickly.

POSTCARDS are quick, brief, easy, and cheap. They can remind individuals of a deadline, provide needed information, ask a question, or set the stage for a telephone call with time, agenda, and names of participants. When you want information or a vote, they can be self-addressed and included with a letter.

LETTERS FROM THE CHAIR are invaluable when the leadership team is spread out "all over the map." They help communicate information and transact business if well organized, specific, and brief. Give dates and places; start each item with an *underlined heading*; give assignments for all to see; tell them what they need to know in order to be effective team members; and enclose a self-addressed postcard for timely, no-hassle responses.

A NEWSLETTER is the single most effective method to keep members informed of organizational news. Only a few people attend all the meetings, activities, conferences, and conventions of a group; even fewer know what the various committees are planning and doing. Even those who attended meetings and events may not be aware of all the important things that took place. A newsletter reaches everyone; a good newsletter tells it accurately and concisely; an outstanding newsletter does all this and more. For many organizations, the newsletter is a primary link to the larger world of other similar and related professional or interest groups. The next few pages are devoted to the art of producing newsletters "par excellence"!

Marks of a Good Newsletter

• Published often enough to keep members informed of the news.
• Covers a broad spectrum of member interests. (See "Forty Ideas" later in this chapter.)
• Written by many different members who have diverse points of view.

- Evaluated by the membership on a regular basis.
- Easy to read layout, spacing, type, emphasis, flow.
- Includes graphics (photos, illustrations, charts, graphs, outlines), used in effective and readable ways.
- Displays a clear masthead with sponsoring organization's name, issue, date, and number.
- Identifies the editor, frequency of publication, address, and the procedure for submitting material for publication.
- Uses copyrighted material from other sources *only* with full permission in writing from the author of original publication.

Ways to Make a Good Newsletter Outstanding

- Typesetting is more readable than typewriting, and word-processing can add a professional touch.
- Non-white paper and two or more colors of ink add eye appeal.
- Printing is more "classy" than mimeographing or dittoing.
- Heavy stock paper prevents bleeding through and gives depth to artwork.
- Clever, original artwork that "fits" the organization helps tell the story and gives the publication power.
- Quality action-photographs taken "on site" make a story believable.
- Selective use of boxes for important announcements (dates, reminders, need for volunteers) adds emphasis.
- Mini-logos of the organization at the end of articles keep your group identity always in sight.
- A variety of border designs when boxing-in items of importance relieves boredom.
- Trimmed edges after folding demonstrate care in preparation.
- "Contents of This Issue" box with page numbers displayed on an outside page invites readers to look inside.
- A masthead banner distinctively representative of the organization proudly displays your identity.

THE MOONSHINERS EYE OPENER
Quarterly Newsletter of the Healthy Order Of Teetotalers
"We Give A HOOT"

Volume IV, No. 2   Spring Issue   April 1, 1999

Using Newsletters for Two-Way Communication

There are three ways to get information from members through your newsletter: cut-outs, inserts, and stick-ons. They can be used for many reasons: questionnaires and surveys; membership application; reservations for activities; change of address; donations; evaluations; nominations for office.

Keep in mind that *any* mailing piece must meet postal regulations for size and format. Currently that means envelopes or card stock at least 3½ x 5 inches and not more than 4½ x 5½ inches. Here are a few more tips:

Cut-Out Response Forms

It takes six steps to return a cut-out: (1) find scissors, (2) cut it out, (3) find an envelope, (4) find a stamp, (5) put it all together, and (6) mail it. Cut-outs also destroy the completeness of the newsletter for future uses of those who save them. them.

Inserts

Inserts must be carefully fastened or folded securely with other pages to prevent them from falling out before they're delivered.

Stick-Ons

Stick-ons make use of a special adhesive that sticks, and yet is easily separated from a newsletter page. It may be the best of the three methods. Pre-stamped, postcard-size stick-ons are very useful when a large response is wanted from the membership. Their easy handling may increase your return percentage.

Newsletter Budgeting

The first rule of producing publications is "It always takes at least twice as long as you planned!" So allow *plenty* of time, then plan for some expense as well.

Your cost analysis should include: *type of paper* (coated stock is magazine-like, expensive, heavy, white); *number of pages* (try to keep the total weight under one ounce...postal rates are high!); *number of colors* (some printers have two-color presses that can produce a two-color result with a single press run — you'll still pay more than for a single ink color); *number of photographs* (and amount of work in enlarging, reshooting, screening); *method of duplicating* (mimeo, ozalid, offset, photocopy. Be sure to get two or three printers to bid on your job); *quality of designing and preparing camera-ready artwork; method of addressing* (hand written, adhesive labels); *labor* (stapling, folding, addressing, stamping, sorting by zip code, bundling, mailing — volunteers or your local lettershop?); *postage* (a *major* cost. Consult the U.S. Postal Service regarding class of mail, bulk mail permits and procedures, pre-sorted first class — for *large* groups, non-profit organization fees and rates — if the IRS defines you as one!).

The cost per copy is the critical figure in considering how many issues the organization will want to publish each year. The cost can be reduced by (1) maximum use of volunteers (labor, typing, etc.), (2) member access to duplication supplies and equipment, and (3) finding the most attractive rate alternatives offered by the U.S. Postal Service.

Evaluating Newsletters

The criteria for evaluation come from goals and objectives set at the beginning of the year. Your newsletter is no exception. If its goals are well defined, it is simple to analyze how close the newsletter came to reaching them: add up column inches, count the various types of articles, photos, contributions. Those original goals and objectives can also be the source of items to use in a newsletter evaluation questionnaire.

Sample Goals/Objectives might include:
- To publish six issues during the year;
- To include a feature story on one member in each issue;
- To summarize the decisions of every meeting of the Executive Board;
- To include an editorial about the club's basic purpose in every other issue; and
- To have 75% of the material submitted by club members.

These are all specific, measurable, and feasible goals. Other ideas will come from the specific needs of your group for an effective communications tool, and from the suggestions we've listed earlier.

While we have given special emphasis to the newsletter in this chapter, bulletin boards, telephones, postcards, and letters from the Chair should all be considered in your overall effort to keep members and the leadership informed. Develop a system that works well for your unique group; keep it sharp through evaluation; and select with care the members who are assigned to make it happen!

Forty Ideas for Newsletter Material

Personal

1. New members...names, addresses, telephone numbers, brief personal background sketches.
2. People news...achievements, travel, family, service to others, job changes.
3. Feature story on a member...interview, editorial, "Faces in the Crowd."
4. Organizational recognition, awards.
5. Letters to the editor...opinions, ideas, questions, suggestions, observations.

Membership Promotion

6. A newcomers column...brief about new members: why they joined; their first impressions.
7. Activities for new members...orientation, special events, get-acquainted socials, newcomers-sponsored programs.
8. "Bring-a-Friend-Free"...popular events, open houses, special programs.
9. Organizational basics...what we're about, what we do, what we've done, why we do what we do.
10. Testimonials..."What the club did for me," getting acquainted.

Activities and Programs

11. Calendar of coming events (try an actual mini-monthly calendar and circle key dates).
12. Highlights of dates and places for future events.
13. Highlights of a recent event.
14. Goals for the year.
15. Progress reports on projects.
16. Community involvement activities and services.

Volunteer Opportunities

17. Need for special talents, services, resources.
18. Committees that need workers.
19. Editorial: why volunteer?

Organizational Management

20. By-laws, policies, standards.
21. Nominations, elections, sample ballots, appointments.
22. Finances, budgets, statements, audits, fund-raising.
23. Convention registration and arrangements.
24. Decisions made at the last meeting.
25. Pro and con arguments on major group issues.
26. Agenda for an upcoming meeting.

Educational/Informational

27. Book or magazine article reviews.
28. Poems, jokes, limericks.
29. Communication skills; effective listening.
30. Legislative analysis; updates; who to write or phone.
31. Managing time.
32. Leadership and skill development.

Membership Services

33. Organizational pamphlets, membership lists.
34. Swap-rent-sell column.
35. Job opportunities.
36. Offerings...share a ride, recipe swap, tip of the month.
37. Use of club equipment and facilities.
38. Announcements of members' new phone numbers or addresses.
39. Lost and found.
40. You-name-it!

Part 3

"Getting Results"

Okay, you're under way! You know something about working with people effectively from Part I. You have had your first meeting, welcomed new members, and developed a communications system in Part II. Now what will you *do* with all this well-oiled machinery?

The "bottom line" of just about every organization is getting things done. Even if the mission or purpose of an organization is to have *fun,* there are some "chores" involved in giving the members what they came for.

In the next several chapters, we'll explore ways to make things happen, getting your members to set goals for your group and work to achieve them. Included are ideas on:
- Setting goals
- Solving problems
- Delegating authority
- Getting the work done
- Keeping records of results
- Letting the public know about them
- Checking up on how it's going

This part covers the real "guts" of your daily leadership function.

READ ON!

11

Setting Goals

Goal setting. It's so important in the life of an organization, and yet many officers are either scared to death or bored stiff at the thought of trying to get members to sit down and agree on what's important. Well, tremble and yawn no more! By the time you've finished this chapter, you'll have the tools you need to conduct a goal setting session that's not only highly effective, but relatively simple and enjoyable for the members as well.

Before getting into the "how," though, it's important to know something more about the "why," "who," "when," and "where" of the goal setting process.

Why Set Goals?

You'll increase motivation (combat apathy) by allowing each member the opportunity to have his/her say in the determination of what the group is going to do. Never forget: *"People will support what they help to create"* and they are likely not to get enthused about projects conceived by a few and "laid" on the membership.

More effective communication results when you let every member know where the group is going. Written goal statements provide a solid framework for planning so that the members will be less inclined to go off on "tangents."

Goals give the group a firm foundation for program/project evaluation. If you have properly written goals and supporting objectives, it will be easy to determine whether or not you have succeeded in doing what you set out to do. (Unless you know where you're going, how will you know when you get there?)

You'll help build a strong sense of teamwork within the membership, and to develop a sense of pride and accomplishment as each goal is achieved. A team can accomplish much more together than individual members working alone.

Who Should Set Goals?

While group leaders should assume responsibility for insuring that the organization *has* written goals (and objectives), goal setting, itself, should be a function of the entire membership. The process should involve all who will be affected by or involved in working to attain the goals.

When Should Goals Be Set?

Goals should be set as early in the year or term of office as possible (it should be the first thing that happens after new officers are elected). Progress toward goals should be evaluated regularly, perhaps monthly or quarterly.

Where Should Goal Setting Take Place?

Goal setting cannot be done in a regular meeting as part of the standard agenda. Good goal setting takes time and concentration. It is best to call a special meeting, or to make it part of a retreat "package," when members can give it careful thought, consideration, and energy.

How Do Groups Set Goals?

Below you'll find a method that can be used by any club or organization in search of the elusive "goal." If you follow this outline, you will very likely come away from a goal setting session with a feeling of accomplishment and satisfaction.

At the end of the chapter, we've provided some supplementary goal setting materials, including: "Criteria for a Good Goal Statement" (plus examples); "Criteria for a Good Objective Statement" (plus examples); and a worksheet you can use to follow through on goal achievement once you've established your basic goals.

STICK 'EM UP: An Innovative Process for Goal Setting

Time Required: 1½ to 3 hours, depending on group size
Materials Required: Pencils and paper for each participant
                          Marking pens (big ones)
Butcher or easel paper, cut into sheets about 18 x 18 inches
Enough stick-on paper dots so that each person has 7 of one
    color and 7 of another color (we use Avery ¾-inch diameter
    self-adhesive labels; they come in boxes of 1,000 in a
    variety of colors).
The Process:
1. Assemble the group, and hand out pencils and paper to each participant.
2. Ask each person to list five things that s/he would like to have the group accomplish within the next six months or a year — whichever suits your timetable best.
3. Ask each person to rank his/her "wish list" from 1 to 5, with 1 being that program, activity, or project he/she MOST wants to see happen, and 5 being the least important.
4. Divide the participants into groups of four, and ask that they share their five ideas with the other group members.
5. Have each person write a goal statement (see "Criteria" later in this chapter) for his/her #1 priority item; have them check the statement with another group member for accuracy and clarity.
6. Have each person announce his/her top-ranked goal to the group while you record the exact wording on butcher paper (with marking pen); tape all goal statements to the wall (around the room).

7. Distribute seven red dots to each group member, explaining that they are PRIORITY ("P") dots.

8. Give participants about 5 minutes to mill around the room, sticking their own priority dots on the posted goals that appeal to them the most. (Note: There are no distribution rules. If a person feels only one goal is important, s/he may stick all of his/her priority dots there; if s/he chooses to split the dots among several goals, that's OK too.)

9. Then distribute seven blue dots to each group member, explaining that they are ENERGY ("E") dots.

10. Give participants about 5 minutes to mill around the room sticking up energy dots, selecting those goals in which each is willing to invest personal energy. (Again, there are no distribution rules. If some wish not to stick up their energy dots, retaining some energy for other activities, even beyond the organization, they should do so. "False deposits" will lead to "false assumptions" about what the group as a whole really wants to accomplish.)

11. Have each participant count the number of priority and energy dots posted on his/her *own* top-ranked goal, and have them write the totals on the sheet (e.g., P = 15, E = 2).

12. Interpreting the Results. As indicated in #8 (above), people relate to goals in two different ways: in terms of how much *priority* they think each of these proposed projects deserves, and in terms of how much *personal energy* they are willing to invest in the accomplishment of each one.

What you're looking for when you're trying to decide which of the posted goals to pursue are those that have high and fairly equal number of "P" dots and "E" dots (e.g., P = 15 and E = 12). These are the goals that the members feel are important to accomplish *and* those for which they're actually willing to work. If people have been honest in their "voting," you should have no trouble finding people to assume responsibility for these "high P, high E" goals. When a goal receives a lot of "E" votes but very few "P's," it means that people really want to do it, but that it's not really critical for organizational survival. (Our experience has been that these goals usually relate to the fun, social aspects of an organization.)

A goal which has a "high P, low E" tally should be discussed at some length, since the members think it's important, but no one really wants to work on it. You may even want to consider hiring someone to get it done, or think about recruiting some new members who have a specific interest or expertise in that particular goal area. If and when you decide to forge ahead on "high P, low E" goals, do so with the acute awareness that volunteers will be hard to come by, and that no one will be particularly enthused about working toward their accomplishment.

13. Find a logical break-point that will give you about 5 to 7 of the most "popular" goals, and announce them to the group.

This entire process will take from 1½ to 3 hours, depending on the size of the group. Usually this is a lot of information for the general membership to digest in one sitting, so you'll probably want to wrap it up at this point — or at least take a break for a while — even though there are still several more steps in the process.

Once you have your 5 to 7 goals, the next step is to establish objectives and a plan of action for each. With the help of supplementary materials provided at the end of this chapter, a small group of members (e.g., your executive committee or steering committee) can do much of the detail work before the next full meeting of the organization. Here's what we suggest:

• If necessary, "clean up" each of the selected goal statements to be sure that they're clear, concise, and understandable (see "Criteria of a Good Goal Statement" coming up).

• Put each goal at the top of a separate sheet of paper, and work with the small group to draft objectives for each one (see "Criteria of a Good Objective Statement" later in this chapter).

• For each objective, a "task assignment worksheet" should be developed. Specify the task and completion date, but leave the "Person Responsible" column blank, and find volunteers at your next meeting.

Here's an abbreviated example of each of these steps:

Goal: To double the membership by the end of the year (June 30).

Objective 1: To conduct, by October 31, a door-to-door membership drive in the downtown business area with the intent of recruiting 50 new members.

Tasks for Objective 1:	Person Responsible	Completion Date
1. Appoint a door-to-door membership drive coordinator	Joe P.	August 1
2. Establish a budget for the drive	Mary	August 1
3. Develop a list of businesses to be approached	Fred	August 15
4. Prepare membership recruitment materials	Mary	August 30
5. Sign-up volunteers to go door to door	Bryan	Sept. 15

With well written and realistic goals, objectives and task assignments, evaluation of the overall success of your term in office should be relatively simple. For the goal above, for instance, you would be able to determine the extent of success simply by comparing the number of active members on the membership roll on June 30 with the number for the year before. Even if you fall short of fully realizing the goals you set, by implementing and following through on this process step-by-step, at least you'll know at what point and by whom the proverbial ball was dropped, and you'll be able to revise your strategy in the future to prevent the same mistakes.

Goal setting. Important? *Essential.* Time consuming? *Sort of.* A good experience for the members? *You bet.* Worth it? *Absolutely.* Give it a whirl.

Criteria for a Good Goal Statement

1. It begins with the word "to" and contains only observable action verbs, such as:

establish	decide	conduct
create	recruit	sponsor
change	train	defeat
present	improve	increase

2. It is a broad statement of what the group wants to accomplish within a relatively long time frame (e.g., a year, a term of office, a semester).
3. It reflects a specific, identifiable result; something that you can evaluate at the end as having accomplished or not.
4. It is realistic, but represents enough of a challenge to make it worth working toward.
5. It ties directly back to the basic purpose (mission) of the organization.

Examples

• "To raise $10,000 for underprivileged children in our community by December 31, 1985."
• "To increase membership participation in organization activities by 25% by the end of the year."
• "To double the number of people in the county who have C.P.R. certification within the next six months."

Criteria for a Good Objective Statement

1. It relates directly to an established goal.
2. It begins with the word "to" followed by an action verb.
3. It specifies a single key result to be accomplished.
4. It is specific: observable or countable (verifiable).
5. It specifies a target date for accomplishment.
6. It specifies the "what" and the "when" needed to accomplish the goal in question.
7. It is realistic and attainable, yet challenging.
8. It is consistent with the resources available, and with organizational rules, policies, and practices.

Examples

• "To fully train three people to do all the publicity for the organization by the end of our term in office."
• "To hold an officers' retreat with 20 people in attendance by August of this year."
• "To sponsor three dances that will net the organization $200 each before the end of the school year."

For Further Reading

• Bancroft, Ed, "Common problems of volunteer groups." *AHGF, 1975,* pp. 111-114.
   Too many goals is cited as a critical problem of volunteer groups, and a workshop design is offered to bring about better planning.

• Fox, Robert S., Lippit, Ronald and Schindler-Rainman, Eva, *Toward a Human Society: Images of Potentiality.* Washington, DC: N.T.L. Learning Resources Corporation, 1973.
   Positive, optimistic approach to establishing and achieving goals with membership group participation. Six approaches are presented to meet the needs of various groups.

• Jones, John E., "Criteria of effective goal-setting: The Spiro model." *AHGF, 1972,* pp. 133-134.
   *S*pecificity, *P*erformance, *I*nvolvement, *R*ealism, and *O*bservability are proposed as criteria for judging goal statements.

• Mink, Oscar G., Shultz, James M. and Mink, Barbara D., *Developing and Managing Open Organizations.* Austin, TX: Learning Concepts, 1979, pp. 117-130.
   Organization goals, effective goal setting, periodic reviews, membership involvement, evaluation, and building consensus are all considered.

• Thomson, Thomas M., "Management by objectives." *AHGF, 1972,* pp. 130-132.
   Stresses need for member involvement in the process of setting goals to gain commitment and quality results. Notes importance of evaluating results and changing goals accordingly.

Goal, Objective and Task Assignment Worksheet

Goal 1:

Objective 1:

Tasks for Objective 1:

Task	*Completion Date*	*Person Responsible*

Objective 2:

Tasks for Objective 2:

Task	*Completion Date*	*Person Responsible*

12

Solving Problems

This chapter presents a broad, generalized ''plug 'em in and let 'er rip'' model for quality decision-making that is drawn from several different sources. We have avoided a lengthy discussion of the philosophical, technical or theoretical aspects of the decision process. (Our assumption here is that those who really want to explore this topic in depth will, with great gusto, dive into the references provided at the end of the chapter.)

But before we go any further, let's be sure to get our terms straight. *Problem-solving* is an individual or collaborative process composed of two different skills: (1) to analyze a situation accurately, and (2) to make a good decision based on that analysis.

In the problem-solving flow chart presented below, boxes 1, 2, and 3 represent the steps involved in analyzing a situation carefully so that you can be sure exactly what the problem *is* before you move ahead with trying to make some decisions about solving it. Boxes 5 to 9 describe the steps involved in decision-making, itself.

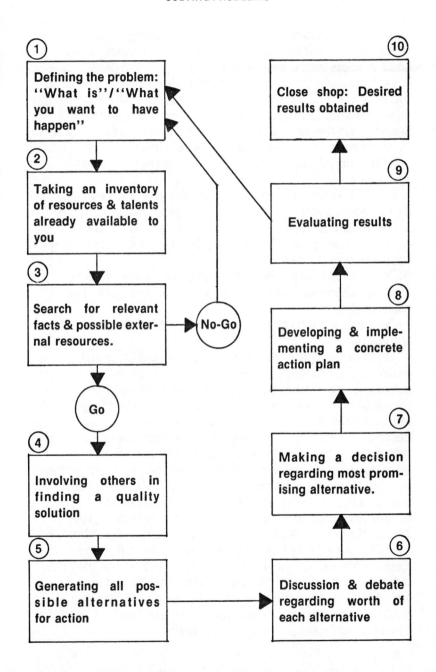

A quick rundown of each of the steps, using an example that may be familiar, may help you better understand the basic process we're describing.

Let's assume that your organization's budget is $1,000 for the year and that $500 of that budget comes from membership dues and $500 is supposed to come from fund-raisers. Six months into the year, you've spent $500, but raised only $25 through your fund-raising activities. Six months to go, and you have only $25 to work with, unless something changes, and soon!!

The first thing to keep in mind is that you don't really have a problem to solve unless you have at least two alternative actions open to you. In this case your alternatives are:

a) You can stop spending and do nothing that costs money for the rest of the year;

b) You can increase the number of dues-paying members;

c) You can increase membership dues, or charge a special assessment;

d) You can work on generating income through fund-raising activities.

This is what Step 1 in the process is all about: clearly defining the problem. "What is," in this case, is that you're out of money. "What you want to have happen" should be a choice of alternatives a, b, c, or d, as decided by the general membership, by consensus. *Consensus* is the decision-making strategy we advocate when the group gets together to choose from among alternatives related to important issues which affect the entire membership. When you use the consensus model, you don't settle for a majority vote or a flip of the coin to determine the outcome. In consensus, you discuss each of the alternatives thoroughly, amend them (if necessary), and find that one alternative that every single member of the group can support to some extent. Everyone need not buy into the solution 100%, but they must make a pledge to work toward its accomplishment and not to oppose it, either publicly or privately, once the decision is made. When you reach consensus, there are no "winners" or "losers," only supporters of the decision.

When you present the choices, let's say the members decide that alternatives "a" and "c" are out of the question, that "b" is impossible, and that "d" is the most plausible alternative they have. It is agreed that at least $300 is needed to finish out the year, so fund-raising it is. On to Step 2.

At this point, you need some information. Which members have experience with or interest in co-ordinating fund-raising events? Who might be able to provide free, low-cost, or at least reasonably priced supplies or services that might help you reach your $300 fund-raising goal? Make a list of both, then move to Step 3.

In Step 3, you might discover that certain days or weekends are "out" in terms of participation by many members, that a competing organization has already planned a certain type of money-making event, that Ed's brother is a printer, that Eileen's son has access to a celebrity in town, and that the Saturday Club is hurting for income and may be willing to negotiate a discount rental price for one or two evenings in the near future.

You've now reached a critical point in the process: "go" or "no go." Based on this example, what you know so far (hypothetically) is this:
• The members want to continue to hold activities.
• They estimate $300 is needed.
• They think that sponsoring fund-raising events is the best way to get the money required to finish out the year.
• Two people have experience in fund-raising; three more people are interested in learning about it.
• Five of the members can provide free, low-cost or reasonably priced supplies or services that may be of assistance.
• You have a line on some significant external resources, and are aware of all of the "facts" that may inhibit or enhance your chances of success.

In the case just described, it looks as though you have enough going for you to "go" with alternative "d"! If, however, you had been unable to come up with these kinds of positive indicators, your decision would have been "no go," at which point you'd want to reconsider alternatives "a" and "b."

O.K.: it's a "go." Who should be involved from here on? All those who have energy, interest or resources to contribute. (The five people who indicated experience/interest in fund-raising, plus the five who have personal resources to offer, plus Ed, plus Eileen. Presto! A committee has been formed, and Step 4 is completed.)

You'll notice that you have not yet decided exactly what kind of fund-raiser is most appropriate. This is the crux of Step 5, now that you have the people with the experience, interest, and resources together. Given what you know so far, the list of alternatives for a committee decision might look something like this (Step 5):

1. A Halloween dance
2. A midwinter banquet
3. An antique auction
4. A swap meet
5. A children's carnival.

This is the real beauty of this process: those who have the resources needed to solve the problem — the committee selected in Step 4 — are the most involved in deciding which is the best way to approach it. For the sake of discussion, let's say they evaluate these options in the light of reality, constraints, and potential for success (Step 6) and choose alternative #1 (Step 7).

This committee is now dealing with a defined goal ("To raise enough money by the end of the year to finance all previously planned organizational activities"), complete with the following objective: "To sponsor a Halloween dance at the Saturday Club on October 31 which will net our group $300."

Step 8, then, is the development of a "task worksheet" (see Chapter 11), and Step 9 is Program Evaluation (see Chapter 21).

If the objective is met, i.e., if you *do* net the $300 you need on the dance, no more fund-raising has to be done, and you move (happily and with relief!) to Step 10. If, on the other hand, only $150 is raised (rats!), you'll need to go back to Step 1 and start over again, re-stating the problem once again in terms of your four alternatives for action ("a," "b," "c," or "d").

The assumptions underlying this approach to problem-solving and decision-making are these:
- People will support what they help to create. Go for consensus.
- Not everyone in the organization has to be actively involved in actually making the decision, but they must have the chance to become involved if they have something to offer: resources, interest, or experience.
- Without a clear statement of the problem, there will be no clear notion of the possible or most appropriate solutions. You must define *exactly* what you want "to have happen."
- Most organizations spend far too little time thoroughly analyzing the situation before moving into the decision-making phase. You must know what resources you have "in your hip pocket" before deciding which solution is potentially the most promising one to pursue.
- You'll want to follow this model "to the tee" only when relatively major problems arise in your group. Problems that affect the well-being or status of a majority of the membership deserve this kind of attention and time; minor problems probably don't.
- This process may be used to discover solutions for a whole range of organizational problems, but it is particularly useful when goals set at the beginning of the year "bog down" or go awry.

Try it. We think you'll like it...a lot.

For Further Reading

- Earley, Leigh C. and Rutledge, Pearl E., "A nine-step problem-solving model." *AHGF, 1980,* pp. 146-151.
  Excellent presentation of a model for group decision-making: define, attack alternatives, test reality, decide, plan action, implement, evaluate, and start a new cycle if necessary.

- Francis, Dave and Young, Don, *Improving Work Groups: A Practical Manual for Team Building.* San Diego, CA: University Associates, 1979, pp. 216-217 and 226-229.

Two exercises: "Effective problem-solving survey," and "How do we make decisions?"

- Gibb, J.R., *Dynamics of Participative Groups: Consensus in Decision-Making.* St. Louis, MO: John S. Swift Co., Inc., 1951, pp. 27-30.

Importance and value of consensus decision-making; seven reasons consensus is not reached; importance of immediacy and gravity of the problem; effective communication; "pitfalls" of debate.

- Janis, Irving L., "Group think." *Psychology Today,* November, 1971.

A classic on the challenges of quality decision-making during the years of the John F. Kennedy administration.

- Ross, Martin B., "Creativity and creative problem solving." *AHGF, 1981,* pp. 124-134.

Barriers to creativity (psychological, cultural, environmental, language, operational rigidity, and habitual ways of seeing situations). Techniques to stimulate creativity (creative problem solving, analogies, problem component analysis, questioning attitude, brainstorming, including outsiders, and a creative climate).

- Sherwood, John J. and Hoylman, Florence M., "Utilizing human resources: Individual versus group approaches to problem solving and decision making." *AHGF, 1978,* pp. 157-162.

When to choose group and when to choose individual approaches; importance of commitment to the solution or acceptance of the decision; importance of quality of the decision.

- Steers, Richard M., *Introduction to Organizational Behavior.* Santa Monica, CA: Goodyear Publishing Co., Inc., 1981.

Primarily a business management approach; sections on decision making and group effectiveness are useful for volunteer organizations.

- Yoes, D.E., "An introduction to PERT or (Now that we are finally agreed on where we want to go, how do we arrange to get there from here?)." *AHGF, 1972,* pp. 135-137.

Program Evaluation and Review Technique is a group analysis and flow-charting procedure. Involves a sequence of necessary events and involves everyone.

13

"Volunteering" Members to Share the Work

Some members volunteer just to volunteer. Other members volunteer to work...and work and work. Every member who volunteers is a potential worker, but s/he will not necessarily jump on every project that comes along or respond every time volunteers are needed. If you believe that every individual is uniquely valuable (of course you do), your calls for volunteers should be tempered with a generous helping of regard for their unique personal motives.

Let's look at ways presidents typically solicit committee workers: "We need about ten people to paint posters Sunday afternoon for our big concert. Will all members interested in helping, please...

...raise your hand;
...sign the sheet being passed around;
...contact me after the meeting;
...get in touch with Delores before Saturday
...show up at the park at 7 a.m."

Which of the above do you think would be most effective in getting volunteers who will both show up and work? Actually none of them is consistently reliable.

Why? Well, for one thing, some people can't resist the attention they get by just raising their hand. It's even more rewarding and more effective when the secretary takes their names down and asks, "Do you have a car or need a ride?" Some will sign a sheet being passed around; at least it's a record of who volunteers. A lucky president will recover the signed sheet at the end of the meeting, but it might come back with less than the ten people required, or even blank! Contacting the president after the meeting to volunteer may be difficult (really almost impossible), since presidents are often busy with all sorts of things after adjournment. What's more, even members who are interested in volunteering may be *more* interested (when the meeting is over) in getting a ride home (or pursuing social interests...). The last alternative may result in no one showing up at the park at all, that is, unless someone contacts likely volunteers directly or by telephone before the work is scheduled to begin.

There *must* be better ways to enlist volunteers and (hold onto your socks!) there are!! Here are five:

• Use the *Membership Information Card* discussed in Chapter 8. When you know the interests, special abilities, and resources of members, and the days and times potential volunteers are most likely to be available, getting a group together is easy. Phoning those available, interested, and skilled in the work to be done is both simple and effective.

• Select a chairperson *before* the meeting from the *Membership Information Card* or from past experience. Once the project leadership has been established, it is easier to get volunteers either at the meeting or by personal contact. "We have an excellent chairperson for the poster painting party Sunday afternoon. Now all we need are some folks who'll help." This removes members' debilitating dread of ending up with total responsibility, and at the same time offers the hope that they may even have some fun.

• Form everyone into small groups at the meeting. Explain the need for a work force, and ask each group to do a "talent search" for poster makers. Suggest they check with individuals directly, regardless of which group they're in, to confirm their willingness to help before presenting their names to the entire membership. This process should take no more than five minutes, it's sort of "festive," and a capable, reliable work group will likely result.

• Make a special effort to get new members involved. They may be looking for ways to meet other members. Phone them for a "Get Acquainted" work party. (What a sneaky idea...)

• Make it a learning experience. For example: "We need some posters for the concert and we have an expert graphic artist who will teach you how to make attractive, *individual* posters. Charlie Creative is a professional artist, and he'll have all materials (paper, paint and brushes) set up in his home Sunday at 2 p.m. Who would like to give 'poster painting' a try?"

In addition to being personally approached, volunteers tend to do better when given "positive notice" by such people as the president, another officer, or the historian taking photographs while they're working. Take them a hot drink when the weather is cold and a cool drink on a hot day. Make it a fun occasion, then say something humorous and personal about the event at the next meeting. "May was our expert on painting borders, George specialized in scissors, Bert was a whiz as 'color coordinator,' Martha was #1 troubleshooter, and Joe kept the coffee flowing without even getting his designer jeans dirty!"

We have emphasized the point that *people support what they help to create.* It is very likely that those volunteers who make a project a success will come from those who were most involved in selecting that project. Think about it. And *don't* point the fickle finger of guilt at the non-volunteers if you didn't really get them involved in deciding on the project in the first place.

There are times when members do not volunteer because they lack confidence in being able to do the job required. When you feel this is holding some members back:

• Pair up the low-confidence member with another who is skilled in the task and interested in helping another member (modeling).

• Plan the work event as an opportunity to learn a new skill. Select or employ someone to give instruction and opportunities for volunteers to get experience and feedback (skill building).

• Provide someone to watch over the performance of volunteers to see that all goes well and to insure the quality of their work (supervision-follow-up).

There are also those who tend to be "loners," the "never-volunteers" who prefer to avoid group work projects, but who do like to work alone. Try designing involvement tasks to suit their particular interests or styles...perhaps technical jobs, such as operating audio-visual projection equipment, photography, managing tickets, mailing newsletters, or computerizing membership data.

And for those "too busy" to volunteer between meetings, search for things that must be done just before, during, and just after meetings.

Believe it or not, there really are those occasions when there's a nasty, dirty or unpopular task to be done — like cleaning up after a banquet or party. Genuine no-fun jobs do come along from time to time, but when there seem to be no easy answers, consider these:

• Resort to pulling names out of a "hat" which includes *all* names (*including* the officers'). Those pulled are responsible for being there and doing the work, or for having a "representative" there. This is a "Russian roulette" type of game that doesn't have the negative impact of coercion or naming people arbitrarily. Be sure to remove their names so they are not "eligible" for the next drawing.

• Divide the membership into "volunteer groups" of 5 to 10 people. Do it according to their residential proximity, type of transportation, randomly or by their own choice. Be sure everyone knows which V-group they're in. Then just pull *group* names out of the "hat."

• Offer them something — a free dinner, tickets to the event, a hot-tub party after the job is done, a gift certificate to somebody's garage sale...or other exciting goodies generated from brainstorming.

• Increase the dues and *pay* people to do the dirty work. (Well, it *is* an option...).

Finally, it is not realistic to expect members to volunteer themselves to work on every project appearing on the calendar. All have a multitude of personal interests and commitments beyond this organization, so don't make them feel guilty when they say "no." It is a *voluntary* membership organization, and that's what makes your leadership role so interesting. *You* volunteered too, remember?

14

Developing Effective Committees

Does anybody like long, long meetings? Probably not, yet one of the most common reasons volunteer organizations *have* drawn-out meetings is that they have not used committees effectively. Endless hours can be saved when committees function properly, when their reports are concise and complete, and when they can answer questions from the floor. The full membership need not waste its time re-doing the committee's job; "another long meeting" can be avoided!

Organizations that base their productivity on committees recognize that a great deal of business must be done between meetings, and that small groups are more effective than large ones in giving careful consideration to a problem.

A committee has several advantages which make its work easier and more effective than its parent organization.

1. *Size:* A small group can meet more easily and more often, deliberate more efficiently, and work more rapidly. Its members get a chance to contribute their best efforts without fighting for "air time." Group members get to know one another and are freer in exchange of ideas.

2. *Isolation:* Removed from the flurry of other business and the bluster of debate, a small committee has "room" to do its work more quietly and effectively.

3. *Freedom of Discussion:* The chairperson is an active participant, individuals can ask questions and bring up other related matters while discussion is going on, and there is no limitation on the number of "speeches" or the length of "debate."

4. *Informality:* There is no need for the constraints and procedures of parliamentary law.

5. *Select Make-Up:* Members can be chosen for their expertise, ability, and interest in the committee's particular assignment. No one need be "just sitting there."

6. *Training:* Committee work can be an excellent officer-training experience for people who aspire to leadership positions.

7. *Discreetness:* Delicate, troublesome, or embarrassing questions may be handled by a committee quietly and privately.

8. *Hearings:* Committees may hold hearings to learn the opinions of members and outside consultants who may be called in as experts. Such counsel may be more readily given to a small group than to the full membership.

With all these advantages, why don't organizations conduct all of their business through committees? Probably because many leaders don't know how to use committees effectively. To get the most out of *your* committees, start them off on the "right foot":

• Give them thorough instructions, including a deadline for getting the job done;

• Select members with diverse ideas and a sincere interest in the job;

• Select a chairperson who is expert in leading informal group discussions (not *necessarily* expert in the *subject* of the committee's work!).

Committees: In General

To function effectively, committees must have members who are chosen for their expertise, ability, and interest in the work to be done. (Review Chapter 13's do's and don'ts about "peopling" committees to insure productivity.)

The chairperson of a committee is the one the organization depends upon to call meetings, get the job done efficiently, and report back to the membership. This person should thoroughly understand the assignment, be committed to doing it, and be especially good at leading informal discussions. Because you'll add members with various good ideas on the subject, you need not select the "most expert" individual to chair the committee.

Whether this person is *elected* by the membership, *appoin-*

ted by the president, or *chosen* by the committee's membership at its first meeting is a matter of judgment. All of the above methods may be used successfully. To be voted into office by the membership can certainly be taken as evidence of their confidence and support, just as appointment by the president is an announcement of trust in one's ability and commitment. There is also the possibility that committee members may work more diligently to produce a superior product with a chairperson they select themselves.

The need for a committee generally develops during the discussion of a problem at a general meeting: *"I move we refer this entire matter to a committee."* (Caution: It can be a "cop out" for the group. Committees aren't *always* the answer!) When seconded and passed, the responsibility for giving directions to the committee and naming its membership and chairperson rests with the organization president, unless the motion states otherwise. For example: *"The committee on Cooperative Neighborhood Gardens will be responsible for developing a plan for neighborhood garden cooperatives throughout the city. We will expect to hear progress reports at every meeting and a final written report on November 15. I'll be talking to those of you who have shown the most interest in this new project, and the committee will be announced at the next meeting."*

The president may ask the membership to help establish objectives for the committee, even before committee members are selected. Brainstorming or discussion in small groups will probably generate many good ideas, and identify potential committee members. Ten minutes of the larger group's time when the committee is appointed can pay big dividends later!

A recorder or assistant chairperson to keep notes is another "must" for a working committee. This person need not know much at all about the subject to be discussed, but s/he should be interested in it, committed to the committee's job, and a team worker. This can be a valuable "entry-level" experience for a "leader-in-training," but the person should be prepared to call and chair a meeting if needed.

Once the duties of the committee have been developed and the members, chairperson and assistant have been appointed, you may want to involve the overall membership of the full group again in helping to "launch" the committee. It's surprising how members will "open up" with good ideas once the committee's membership has been announced (and they no longer feel they might be "fingered" to serve!). Brainstorm the question, "How can we help this new committee get started?" The committee will probably get a flood of ideas and the sense that the organization really supports what they'll be doing and wants them to succeed. Use care, however, if you're going to a committee *because* the larger group had no ideas!

Committee Meetings (See also Chapter 15 on "Informal Discussions")

The chairperson should have the following materials at the first committee meeting...
...the motion that formed the committee in the first place;
...a complete statement of the committee's duties and powers;
...the names, addresses and telephone numbers of committee members;
...special instructions and restraints, such as pertinent organizational policies, guidelines related to the expenditure of funds, and rules governing the use of resources;
...copies of correspondence and paper relating to the task assigned to the committee; and
...information about the report that's desired and the date already set for its presentation.

Before committee members plunge into the guts of the problem, and start "squaring off" on their differences, the chairperson should help the group organize itself into a team. (The team-building ideas of Chapter 5 may help.) Primarily s/he should work to...
...create an informal atmosphere that is free, creative, and encouraging so that all may contribute openly.

...help members get to know one another on a first-name basis, sharing the experiences and knowledge that each one brings to the committee.

...gain agreement on committee procedures: when and where to meet, time and length of meetings, assignment of tasks to be done, and sharing telephone numbers for easy contact between meetings.

Next, the committee needs to get a good handle on how each member views the assignment. The chair should let members get their differences out in the open, and as the group moves along, keep them focused on the committee task. (Many leaders make the mistake of jumping at the first solution suggested, when it may appeal to only one or two people, or to the bolder ones.)

A collection of mature, able people does not necessarily make a mature, able committee! Newly-formed groups are often very immature. They may become productive or stay impotent. The committee chairperson should help the group mature by giving them enough "space" that they'll begin to take on more *group* responsibility. Small groups tend to have a "life cycle" of their own, and few progress to genuine task work until they have gone through some "interpersonal chores." Members have to learn about each others' behavior in the group, and pay attention to the ways they relate to each other. The leader should *not* intervene to "smooth differences," but should interrupt non-productive exchanges and ask members to reflect on what's going on. Do this just a few times, and the members will begin to monitor their own behavior. As they recognize "what's happening" at the human communication level, they can use that insight to further their task work. They'll be pleased with their progress as they "mature"!

As the group becomes productive in its work on the assignment, the discussion leader should help the committee to build on the knowledge, skills, and other resources that lie within its members. Frequently groups have potential resources which are never discovered because a few members are too busy fighting among themselves to notice.

Reporting Back

Committee reports become official organization records and should be done with care. If they contain complex material that needs membership understanding before full approval, copies or summaries should be distributed to every member, projected on a screen, posted in the meeting room, or presented in the newsletter.

Important reports should be given enough meeting time to get membership feedback, discussion, and support for the recommendations. And isn't that why the group appointed a committee in the first place?

Final reports should be clear and concise, with no sentence or paragraph which does not help answer the question, "What do I hope to accomplish with this report?" The best report contains all the necessary information but no unnecessary details:

- State the subject or committee assignment.
- Set your conclusions or recommendations clearly apart from the body of the report.
- State the facts clearly and simply. Avoid long, involved sentences.
- Put detailed figures, graphs, tables in supplements or appendices.
- Give the names of the committee members, the signature of the chairperson, and the date.

All committee reports require some sort of action by the general membership.

1. *Adoption:* The committee chairperson generally makes this motion: *"I move the adoption of this report."* It is seconded and, if passed, the organization accepts *everything* within the report: its recommendations, resolutions, findings, or conclusions. The motion may be defeated, however, or any one of the following actions may also be taken:

2. *File:* The report is simply received and included in the organization's records without opinion or action.

3. *Postpone:* Discussion on the report is delayed to a more convenient or appropriate time.

4. *Return:* The matter is given back to the committee for more information or work.

5. *Refer:* The work is given to an officer, the board of directors, or another committee for further study.

6. *Substitute:* The committee's efforts are rejected in favor of a minority report.

7. *Divide:* Parts of the report are accepted, other parts are not.

Committee records, minutes, are property of the committee and do not become organizational records. They are generally destroyed when the committee's job has been completed. This is an important point, because committee minutes are generally quite detailed, and often confidential.

Standing Committees

Standing committees generally fulfill continuing needs of the organization and are established in the by-laws. Some typical standing committees are: finance, membership, program, publicity, awards, and elections. Some standing committees are elected by the membership; others are appointed by the president, by the executive board, or by a combination of these methods. Their procedures are very similar to those described above for ''special task'' committees.

Ex-officio members of committees are so-named because their membership is established automatically ''by virtue of their office.'' The basic reason for having ex-officio members of committees is to connect the work of the committee with the overall goals of the organization. Ex-officio members have all the rights, duties, and responsibilities of other members. Their membership automatically terminates with their terms of office; the new office-holders become the ex-officio committee members.

Blue Ribbon Committees and Task Forces

A ''blue-ribbon'' committee is sometimes so-named to give

unique importance to a group made up of individuals with special qualifications.

A "task force" is a special kind of committee assigned the responsibility, power, and authority to take action to carry out a specific job. A task force can be appointed either by the organization to get something done (pronto!), or it may be appointed by a higher authority to take action *against* a subunit of a larger organization, such as a local chapter of a national organization. Because of its unusual authority, the task force is held accountable to the general membership for any action taken.

As we bring to a close this chapter, we want to emphasize the value (indispensability!) of committees to the productive lives of organizations. In most groups, general meetings are weeks or even months apart, and last only an hour or two. Good, solid working committees during the interim make the general meetings both challenging and productive. Only when committees know precisely what they are to do, and only when committees are made up of knowledgeable and interested members and a well-trained chairperson, can you expect your organization to thrive. When committees really "work" — in every sense of the word — the organization will be rewarded with members who are justly proud of their group's accomplishments!

For Further Reading

• Auer, J. Jeffery and Ewbank, Henry Lee, *Handbook for Discussion Leaders.* New York: Harper and Brothers, 1954, pp. 71-83.
    Sections on the role of the leader in group discussion and the role of the committee chairman are directly relevant to committee process. An excellent reference.

• Bradford, Leland P., *Making Meetings Work: A Guide for Leaders and Group Members.* La Jolla, CA: University Associates, 1976.
    Excellent reference for committee processes during meetings. Helps committees to function effectively and get their jobs done.

• Hall, D.M., *Dynamics of Group Action.* Danville, IL: The Interstate Publishers and Printers, 1960, pp. 10-29.
    The chapter "Why groups fail" (atmosphere, people, roles, organization) is especially relevant to committee work. A good general reference.

• Robert, Henry M., *Robert's Rules of Order Revised.* New York: William Morrow and Co., Inc., 1971, pp. 206-235.
    The section on committees and boards details structure, types of committees, and procedures for committee reports. More concerned with "correctness" than process.

• Sturgis, Alice F., *Learning Parliamentary Procedure.* New York: McGraw-Hill Book Co., 1953, pp. 244-270.
    Excellent chapters on "Committees and their work" and "Committee reports."

15
Leading Informal Discussions

It is difficult to imagine a volunteer organization thriving without taking advantage of the richness of informal discussion. In small informal groups everyone is expected to actively participate. There is freedom from the constraints of parliamentary procedure, the informal atmosphere releases the creativity of members, and people can talk directly to one another to develop understanding. Informal discussions are at the heart of committee meetings and small group problem-solving during business meetings and can even kick into gear when the entire membership is convened as a "Committee of the Whole" to discuss a matter informally. Each of these situations is presented later in this chapter.

What Is an Informal Discussion?

Informal discussion at its best might be described as "organized spontaneity." Much more than just sitting around talking and hopping from one topic to another, informal discussions which are *planned, purposeful*, and *centered* on a particular topic or problem have a definite objective to work toward, and function under the low-key guidance of a designated leader selected from within the group.

Size and Group Arrangement

To allow everyone to actively participate, informal discussions are most successful when limited to not more than fifteen or twenty people. Good eye contact among all participants is essential, therefore arranging chairs in a circle is ideal. Note the following seating arrangements:

(a) In this circle people can be seated at a table or in comfortable lounge chairs in a living room.

(b) This larger circle still allows everyone to have direct eye contact with everyone else.

(c) In this arrangement there are three on a side; the center person *prevents* eye contact between the other two.

(d) The longer the table, the greater the problem. For example, twelve of the twenty people in this arrangement are "blockers" of effective communication! An alternative in this setting is to ask each person to stand at the end of the table while speaking,...but *that* defeats the values of informality and spontaneity. "Conference tables," slightly rounded on the long sides, improve this situation slightly, but still prevent effective "same side" eye contact.

Because direct eye contact and attention are so important to understanding the meaning of a message, you may want to consider the advantages of a predetermined seating arrangement around a table, complete with name cards. This may signal an air of formality when people arrive, but that can be easily overcome with an atmosphere of friendliness and informality. For example, try seating people who generally seem to have difficulty understanding one another directly opposite one another. Likewise, those who like to whisper to their neighbors should be placed between others who will not tolerate being distracted. Very good friends, spouses, and car-pool buddies can be split up to free them from the temptation of creating "private agendas."

(e) A better alternative might be to move the table(s) out of the way and just form a circle of chairs. By so doing, every person can see the speaker regardless of position in the circle, and the speaker can see everyone else.

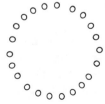

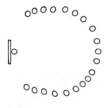

(f) When you plan to use visual aids, a U-shape is an excellent arrangement, with an easel, chalkboard or projection screen at the open end.

(g) Almost all meeting rooms seem to be set up with chairs in columns and rows. This works fine when, individually, members are interacting with a speaker or when they're individually looking at material projected on a screen, but it doesn't do much for interaction among the members! Sitting in a chair viewing the backs of others' heads is not very enlightening; neither is squirming around to get a glimpse of the person whose voice you are hearing. If you find yourself stuck with this sort of arrangement, don't despair! Three ways to make such seating work are described later in this chapter: small (buzz) groups, brainstorming, and the Personal Agenda.

Planning in advance will increase the chances for success of an informal discussion. It doesn't "just happen." Responsibility for taking the initiative rests with the person who will lead the discussion, and the plan will depend on the situation.

If an important decision must be made at the next meeting and the membership lacks the necessary background information to discuss the matter knowledgeably, the plan might be:

...To arrange for four interested members to research different aspects of the issue.

...To inform members that this will be a *special meeting* with nothing else on the agenda, and that the membership will discuss the issue as a *"Committee of the Whole."*

...To have the four researchers sit in front at the meeting and be given five minutes each to report their findings.

...To ask the membership to interact with the research team with questions and comments to insure full understanding.

...To form the membership into a *"Committee of the Whole"* to discuss the matter informally and vote on the action it wishes to take.

...To call to order the meeting of the organization to vote on the report of the *Committee of the Whole."*

If time permits, the above matter could be referred to a special committee of members to study the available facts and to recommend action to the overall membership. The report of this special committee can be discussed informally by a vote of the membership to do so. Following this, a vote on the committee recommendation can be taken.

Mailing out material for members to study before the meeting will often prepare them for active involvement in the informal discussion.

A statement of the problem together with factual information about it and a check-list of several alternative actions can be distributed at the meeting and will start them thinking. The informal discussion that follows will probably start without that usual "long pause" when you say, "What do you think we ought to do?"

Here is an example of a prepared statement-check list to be used to stimulate an informal discussion:

> The County Department of Parks and Recreation
> has asked us to endorse a proposal to make all
> school grounds in the county available for summer

recreation activities. The plan provides for individuals and organizations to assist by making
donations and recruiting volunteer workers to
maintain the grounds and facilities, to patrol the
building areas, and to supervise the areas when
recreation will take place. They have set a goal of
$50,000 and 5,000 person-hours of patrolling and
supervision. *Please mark the following
alternatives with your first, second, third choices.*
    (a) Endorse the proposal and contribute $500.
    (b) Endorse the proposal and pledge 100 hours.
    (c) Endorse the proposal, contribute $500
        and 100 hours.
    (d) Endorse the proposal without contri-
        butions or pledge.
    (e) Do not endorse the proposal.

Leading the discussion can be tricky business, since you
must assist the group in accomplishing its objective and still
remain in the background. It is being both a good listener
and a good observer: understanding what is being said and
sensing what is going on. Although it helps to know something about the topic, it's more important to know when to
intervene and how to help the group move forward. The art
of intervention, once you've decided it's necessary, comes
primarily from being skilled at asking questions. If you can
deal with nonproductive situations by raising questions
instead of making statements, you're on your way to
becoming a red-hot discussion leader.

Here are some ways:

- To bring a gross generalization down to earth...
  "Can you give us a specific example of your point?"
  "Your general idea is helpful, but I wonder if it can't be
  more concrete?"
  "Can anyone describe a case when this was so?"
- To deal with someone who is talking too much...
  "Is there anyone who hasn't spoken who has some ideas
  they'd like to express?"
- To cut off a long-winded speaker...

"While we're on this point, let's hear from some of the others. Can we save your other point until later?"
• To break up an argument...
"I think we all know how Jasper and Molly feel about this. Now, who else would like to comment?"
• To clarify a confusing statement...
"I wonder if what you are saying isn't...?"
"As I understand it, what you've said ties in with our topic something like...."

Other Tips for Low-Key Discussion Leaders

• Establish a friendly and positive atmosphere. Become one of the group, be at ease, and smile graciously.
• Be certain everyone knows everyone else by name, and that they know something about each other that relates to the topic to be discussed.
• State the topic and objective of the discussion clearly, including any time constraints.
• Make *your* role clear! "I'm certainly not an expert on this topic,...but I hope I can help us reach our objective in the time available with an occasional comment or question to keep us on track and to make it easy for everybody to speak up."
• If the discussion is likely to get complex, have someone keep a record of important points and decisions. Use newsprint, a chalkboard, or projection equipment if it will help.
• Keep the discussion balanced when there are different points of view. "We've heard several reasons in favor of the idea, are there any reasons to oppose it?"
• Summarize progress when needed, "Am I correct in assuming that these are the main points that have been made ..., ..., ...?"

Buzz Groups

Have you ever noticed that people who come to a meeting together also sit together? What's more, they tend to think alike, and to agree on most things. If you simply arrange small discussion groups so they are made up of people with *different* ideas and values, you have improved their chance of becoming productive, and it will give the membership some variety, some new acquaintances. This can be done simply by rearranging chairs from rows to small circles, and seeing to it that you break up the "cliques" in the process.

If there are 100 people in a room in groups of five, 20 people will be talking at the same time, and close to 100 will be actively participating. With rows and columns, only one person can talk and 99 are "just there" in various states of involvement and consciousness. Thus, by creating small discussion groups you have markedly increased the level of participation at the meeting, and are likely to get better task results as well!

Buzz groups need to be told what to do, *before* you form them. Once small groups are formed, you'll literally lose control of the meeting temporarily, due to people moving around and talking. So, start by telling them what to do and how much time they have to do it, and asking them to select a person to summarize their key points and report for the group.

A word of caution! In a large group, be sure you have a microphone and speaker system set up to regain control of the meeting when you need it; the level of conversational noise will be a new experience for you the first time you try it!

Buzz groups have proved very effective for a number of common meeting situations:
• Converting goals into ideas for action
• Making group decisions
• Evaluating a meeting or activity
• Nominating officers
• Selecting activities or planning programs
• Interacting with speakers
• "Caucusing" during meeting recess
• Maintaining continuity — social or task — after a meeting.

Brainstorming Ideas

Brainstorming is an excellent process for encouraging spontaneity, and getting imaginative ideas from your members in an environment void of judgment or censure. It works well using buzz groups. There should be at least five or six people involved in each group, but, if need be, this method can also be used in groups as large as 20 or 25.

Five basic rules must be rigidly observed when you brainstorm, and it's important to make them *very* clear at the outset:

1. Every idea presented must be positive.
2. Every idea should be stated briefly.
3. No comments will be allowed on any idea presented. Criticism of ideas presented is absolutely forbidden.
4. Everyone is encouraged to speak up and to express ideas regardless of how ''off the wall'' they may seem.
5. Everyone is encouraged to present ideas as rapidly as they come to mind.

When all ideas have been listed (or your allotted time is up) the originator of each idea explains it in more detail. After all ideas are fully explained, the group selects the best (in priority order) by voting, and the most popular are given further consideration by the entire membership.

The Personal Agenda

The Personal Agenda is useful at the beginning of a meeting or informal discussion to give all members the opportunity to speak to the entire group about their concerns and priorities. Most people *do* like to talk...to hear themselves. This process gives them a *license* to talk...and they enjoy it! It is effective in determining the interests of the members, and gives everybody the experience of discovering the high priorities among the entire membership. The ideal group size is 15-20, although it may be used with groups as large as 30 by shortening the time given each individual.

• Arrange the group in a circle with everyone facing the center.

• Inform the group that each person will be given the opportunity to do *one* of three things:
   1. Ask a question to get factual information
   2. Ask for help in solving a problem
   3. Make a statement
• Make it clear that participants must choose to do only one of the above and that they will be given only a minute or two (depending upon the size of your group and the total time available) in which to pose their question or make their statement, and receive feedback from the group. When the group begins giving feedback, individuals should be encouraged to take notes on the information or help they receive.
• Begin with any person who is ready with an item, and call "time" promptly.
• Repeat the process until everyone in the group has had an opportunity to speak.

The Personal Agenda gives everyone in the group two good experiences: that of being helped by others in the group and that of helping others by sharing information with them. *And* it gives the officers a chance to become aware of those issues that are of major concern to members.

Whoever is facilitating the exercise should do just that— keep time and keep things moving! The facilitator should *not* get involved in the content of what is being said, except perhaps to clarify misunderstandings if necessary.

A Checklist for Evaluating Informal Discussions

1. Seating was arranged so all could see one another
2. Advance planning was complete
3. Purpose was clear
4. Discussion started quickly
5. Atmosphere was informal
6. Leadership was skillful and "Low Key"
7. Participation was total and active
8. Participation was balanced
9. Contributions were relevant
10. Conflicts were worked through, not avoided

For Further Reading

- Auer, J. Jeffery and Ewbank, Henry L., *Handbook for Discussion Leaders.* New York: Harper and Brothers, 1954, pp. 66-90.
  The section "The leader of group discussion" is an excellent resource for informal discussion leadership.
- Benne, Kenneth D. and Muntyan, Bozidar, *Human Relations in Curriculum Change* (selected readings). New York: The Dryden Press, 1951, pp. 145-191.
  Section B, "Helping groups to improve their operation," is especially relevant to informal discussions. Other parts on diagnosing group difficulties, the work of the discussion group leader, improving group meetings, and group self-evaluation are also quite helpful.
- Cathcart, Robert S. and Samovar, Larry A., *Small Group Communication: A Reader.* Dubuque, IA: William C. Brown Co., Publishers, 1970.
  Excellent conceptual reference for the serious leader of informal, small-group discussions. The authors of the 41 articles are among the "Who's Who" in small-group communication and process.
- Gibb, J.R., Platts, Grace N. and Miller, Lorraine, *Dynamics of Participative Groups.* St. Louis, MO: John S. Swift Co., 1951.
  Excellent reference. Practical ideas and applications of basic principles in informal discussion settings.
- Gulley, Halbert E., *Discussion, Conference, and Group Process.* New York: Holt, Rinehart and Winston, 1964.
  Valuable general reference covering every aspect of discussion: nature of discussion, achieving group goals, leadership functions, special problems of leadership, evaluation.
- Hall, D.M., *Dynamics of Group Action.* Danville, IL: The Interstate Printers and Publishers, Inc., 1960.
  A down-to-earth book of theory and practice with application to informal small-group discussion. The chapter, "How to get participation," is excellent.
- Lawson, John D., *When You Preside.* Danville, IL: The Interstate Printers and Publishers, Inc., 1980, pp. 3-16.
  Effective group discussion, the effective leader, special competencies of the leader, and the roles of the leader, recorder, observer, consultant, and group members are discussed.

16

Presiding at Business Meetings

Meetings (meetings, and more meetings!) are inevitable in volunteer organizations. If you work at it, meetings *can* be fun and interesting, contributing much to the spirit of a group. At their worst, meetings can be deadly dull, an ego trip for leaders, and a big factor in member apathy.

Members should be the "very important persons" *during* a meeting; the leadership team should take responsibility for *setting* the stage, not "hogging" it. Planning, notifying members, arranging facilities, greeting folks, and getting the meeting started are all part of the leadership job. From there on, the session belongs to the members, with help from leaders *as needed* to get the job done!

In this chapter, we'll take a look at "formal" business meetings for relatively "informal" volunteer membership organizations. Our emphasis will be on when, where, and how to make your business meetings effective, flexible, and fun.

How Formal Should a Meeting Be?

There are certain customs about so-called "formal" meetings, although the level of formality varies considerably from group to group and task to task. The meetings of elected officials (such as school boards, city councils and public agencies) are traditionally very formal. Private fraternal orders, service clubs, professional organizations, and some nationally-affiliated groups also have traditions and rituals that tend to formalize their meetings.

Volunteer organizations tend to be more formal when the membership is large, time is limited, meetings are infrequent, business is serious, and the agenda is long. Since there are excellent reference books available on very formal meetings (see bibliography at the end of this chapter), we'll leave it to those readers who need such special information to seek it there. Let's take a look at the business meetings of more "usual" voluntary groups.

Their Perfect Rights

Volunteer organizations are, in fact, "owned" by the membership. *Members* make it all possible. They create by-laws and standing rules, elect officers, approve budgets and financial policies, and make decisions. Members can overrule decisions of the presiding officer, replace him/her, and even vote to dissolve the organization. The authority and power of the presiding officer is delegated *from* the membership. Organizational success requires leadership on the part of everybody...those who are elected and those who do the electing.

Everyone comes into a meeting with unique personal experiences and perceptions. No one person has *the* best idea or solution. Quality is the product of everyone working together. One of the joys of group work is that the best solutions do not necessarily come from those who have spoken loudest and longest! Very often, quieter members have valuable ideas and accurate perceptions. Those who voice disagreement should be welcomed and recognized as potential contributors of creativity and higher quality solutions.

A BILL OF RIGHTS FOR MEMBERS

Every member has an investment in the success of the organization; therefore he/she has a right to:
1. Be informed about every meeting's purpose, date, time, and place.
2. Expect meetings to start on time. (Starting late rewards the stragglers, punishes those who arrive on time, and creates an atmosphere of uncertainty from the outset. It also wastes a lot of valuable time!)
3. See the agenda before the meeting starts in a handout, on a chalkboard, on newsprint, or projected on a screen.
4. Ask questions about any item on the agenda, and propose changes before the agenda is approved. (Some organizations have specific "standing rules" about procedures for adding agenda items.)
5. See and hear what's going on, and be heard when speaking.

6. Understand the meaning of every proposed parliamentary action and what their options are in relation to it.
7. Have all the facts, alternatives, and consequences presented openly, and the opportunity to discuss every item before voting.
8. Participate in the process of selecting officers, representatives, and those who chair committees.
9. Exercise full and free discussion of every item presented for a group decision.
10. Have all the information available to any other member or officer.

Preparing the Agenda

The agenda is the "blueprint" for a meeting, a systematic plan for the sequential conduct of business. Here is the standard order of business generally followed by formal organizations:
1. Call to order.
2. Roll call or quorum count.
3. Minutes: reading, correction, approval.
4. Officer reports.
5. Standing committee reports.
6. Special committee reports.
7. Unfinished (old) business.
8. New business.
9. Announcements.
10. Adjournment.

Volunteer organizations are usually more flexible with rules about the agenda, believing that unnecessary formality stifles spontaneity and enjoyment. We agree. Informality *will* work, and switching traditional agenda items around occasionally is often what members want. Some of the best new ideas, those which would generate lots of membership involvement and discussion, are often treated hurriedly by bored and exhausted members by the time the agenda gets to "New Business"! Members should be encouraged to speak right up and suggest changes before the agenda is approved.

Try making your agenda "thought-provoking" so people will know a little more about what *really* is coming up. For example: rather than simply a dry *"Membership Committee Report,"* on the agenda, try *"Membership Committee:* (a) Membership brochure: $400; (b) Installment payment of dues."

The Presiding Officer: Five Major Responsibilities

The presiding officer of a business meeting has five major responsibilities:

1. *To initiate items or proposals* for members to consider, perhaps describing a need or program idea to the group and suggesting action, or receiving a committee report and calling for a motion to take action on its recommendations.

2. *To facilitate discussion and action* so that it's easy for members to conduct the business which has brought them together. A two-hour meeting *can* seem like sixty minutes if you...

...*Keep things moving.* Set an example with brief, clear, and concise explanations; ask others to do the same. Your job isn't to give facts. (If information is needed, arrange for your vice-president to give it.)

...*Turn over the chair.* When you feel you *must* speak about an issue, ask the vice president to serve as the presiding officer until the motion has been disposed. ("Call on" people to make reports; don't "turn over the chair" to them.)

...*Use your secretary/recorder effectively.* Don't try to remember the exact wording of motions. Ask the secretary to get it straight; you can direct your full attention to the involvement of members.

...*Keep your eyes open.* Watch members for non-verbal clues such as readiness to speak or indications of agreement or disagreement with what's going on or being discussed.

...*Use your authority.* You carry much of the responsibility for deciding what goes on, who gets the floor to

speak, when to press for a vote, in many ways even
whether a motion is passed or defeated. Don't be afraid
to trust yourself or to use your gavel.

...*Handle business by general consent where appropriate.*
If the discussion is all positive, bring the matter to a close.
"It seems that we are in general agreement that we '--------.'
Are there any objections? Hearing none, it is so ordered."

3. *To orient and guide the group* in the conduct of its business.
Parliamentary procedure is a language of its own, and if even
a few members don't speak or understand it, your role is to
act as interpreter. Everyone has a right to know what's going
on and what their options are at any point in the parliamentary process. You may say, "This motion can be discussed, amended, referred to a committee, or perhaps you are
ready to vote on it. It requires a two-thirds vote to pass. What
is your pleasure?" Guide the membership past parliamentary
pot-holes without putting down or intimidating anyone with
your parliamentary wisdom.

4. *To bring about free and complete discussion* of all
questions and to act as a mediator if debate gets aggressive.
Here are a few simple guidelines:

...Keep discussion balanced, alternating speakers for and
against motions.

...Give every member a chance to speak once on a motion
before anyone is permitted to speak twice.

...Keep speakers on the subject: "Thanks, Fred. The
question we're discussing is... Is there any further
discussion on that question?"

...Divide large meetings into small groups to give everyone
a chance to speak, or if some members are too shy to speak
to a crowd.

...Write the motion on a chalkboard or use a projector to
keep the discussion focussed, reduce extraneous comments, and shorten the meeting.

...Suggest a motion to postpone or refer to a committee
when the subject is complex or when more facts are needed.

5. *To keep business orderly* through "informal"
parliamentary procedure. Not only for "parliaments," the
generally accepted rules of procedure, applied fairly and

flexibly, can help any group conduct necessary business more efficiently.

Knowing What to Do with a Motion

Some things you should know about motions:

1. A motion should be made and seconded before any discussion starts. If a matter should be discussed and no one is prepared to make a motion on it, ask for a motion to discuss it informally until a main motion develops.

2. Be certain motions are stated clearly, concisely, completely, and in the affirmative. (Collaborate informally with the maker of the motion as necessary until it meets these requirements, then make sure the secretary has it straight for the record.) After it is seconded, repeat it to the membership for discussion. Some organizations require motions to be presented in writing. While annoying to some, this procedure forces the motion-maker to clarify his/her exact wording before the item can be discussed.

3. The maker of the motion should be given the privilege of speaking on the motion first, to explain the proposal.

4. Only one main motion may be considered at a time.

5. If a motion to amend is made and seconded, the proposed amendment must be voted upon before a vote is taken on the main motion.

6. A main motion may be changed without being formally amended by another motion if the maker of the main motion accepts the change as a "friendly amendment."

7. The word "question" has many meanings: "I'm ready to vote."..."I'd like to ask a question."..."I call for the question." ("Let's vote!")..."I move the Previous Question." ("Let's close debate and vote immediately!")..."Are you ready for the Question?" ("Are you ready to vote?") In parliamentary law, the word "Question" refers to the matter being discussed. It is common to hear such phrases as "The Question is..." or "What is the Question before the House?" You may need to clarify this "question" for *your* group from time to time.

8. To bring a motion to vote, the leader says, ''Are you ready
for the question?'' (Members are saying ''yes'' when they
respond with the word ''question!'' Any objections should
be honored unless a formal motion to close debate has been
approved by the required two-thirds majority). If the group
has no objection, say, ''The Question has been called. All
those in favor say 'Aye'; all those opposed say 'Nay'. The
motion is carried (or defeated).'' Rap the gavel once to indicate
that the decision has been made.
9. All votes take a simple majority except those that inhibit
the right of members to speak. These motions require a two-
thirds vote:
   ...vote immediately (''Previous Question'')
   ...limit debate or extend the time limit on debate
   ...object to considering a question
   ...close nominations
   ...postpone to a definite time by a special order
   ...suspend the rules
10. Whenever a vote requires a two-thirds majority, ask for a
hand vote or a standing vote. (It's impossible to *hear*
two-thirds, anyway!) Unless the group's by-laws define them
differently: ''majority vote'' is more than half of those voting
(do not count abstentions); ''two-thirds vote'' is two-thirds of
the votes cast (do not count abstentions).
11. Unless the by-laws specify otherwise, the chairperson may
vote on every issue or may choose to vote only to swing the
outcome one way or the other.
12. Motions are *ranked* and placed in *categories:* (See the
chart at the end of this chapter for a complete table of motions.)
   ...*Main motions* bring items of business before the group
   for action. They have the lowest rank: any other motion can
   legally be made when a main motion is on the floor.
   ...*Subsidiary motions* amend, postpone, table, limit debate
   or refer the main motion (e.g., to Committee). These are
   the second lowest in rank and only take precedence over a
   main motion.
   ...*Incidental motions* pertain to the method of conducting
   business: point of order, parliamentary inquiry, division of

the assembly, or withdrawing a motion. They take precedence over both main motions and subsidiary motions.

...*Privileged motions* require immediate action of the membership to recess or adjourn. They rank above all other motions and can be made whenever any other motion is being considered.

13. A ''Quorum'' is the number of members eligible to vote that are required to be present in order to transact business legally. The number required for a quorum is generally stated in the by-laws of the organization.

14. A ''Parliamentarian'' can be handy when the details start piling up in a heated business meeting, even if you think you have parliamentary procedure ''wired.'' The parliamentarian is the president's assistant, and conversations between the two should be private.

Ten Ways to Shorten Your Meetings

Want to get folks out the door on time? Here are some ''tried and true'' aids:

1. Start on time.
2. Don't talk too much.
3. Don't call for committee reports when no one is there to report--or when the report is not ready.
4. Before the meeting, ask each person on the agenda how much time will be needed, then appoint a timekeeper to hold them to it.
5. Thank people who minimize unnecessary repetition or irrelevancy.
6. Interrupt speakers if necessary to get debate back on track; summarize the major pros and cons made so far.
7. Put motions or topics on a chalkboard, newsprint, or screen; make sure all pro and con arguments are clear.
8. Require officers to set examples with concise reports, visual aids, and handouts.
9. Post or distribute minutes, (don't read them); study and correct them with the secretary.
10. Require motions to be presented to the secretary in writing as soon as they are proposed.

PRINCIPAL RULES GOVERNING MOTIONS

Order of precedence	Can interrupt speaker?	Requires a second?	Debatable?	Amendable?
I. PRIVILEGED MOTIONS				
1. Adjourn	no	yes	no	no
2. Recess	no	yes	no	no •
3. Question of Privilege	yes	no	no	no
II. SUBSIDIARY MOTIONS				
4. Postpone Temporarily (Lay on the table)	no	yes	no	no
5. Vote Immediately (Previous question)	no	yes	no	no
6. Limit Debate	no	yes	no	yes •
7. Postpone Definitely	no	yes	yes •	yes •
8. Refer to Committee	no	yes	yes •	yes •
9. Amend	no	yes	yes	yes
10. Postpone Indefinitely	no	yes	yes	no
III. MAIN MOTIONS				
11. (a) A General Main Motion	no	yes	yes	yes
(b) Specific Main Motions				
Reconsider	yes	yes	yes	no
Rescind	no	yes	yes	no
Resume Consideration	no	yes	no	no
Create Orders	no	yes	yes •	yes •
V. INCIDENTAL MOTIONS•				
Appeal	yes	yes	yes	no
Point of Order	yes	no	no	no
Parliamentary Inquiry	yes	no	no	no
Withdraw a Motion	no	no	no	no
Suspend Rules	no	yes	no	no
Object to Consideration	yes	no	no	no
Division of a Question	no	no	no	no
Division of Assembly	yes	no	no	no

• No order of precedence among themselves. Each motion decided immediately.

Vote required?	Applies to what motions?	Motions can have what applied to it (in addition to withdraw)?	Can be renewed?
majority	no other motion	no other motion	yes•
majority	no other motion	amend•	yes•
no vote	no other motion	no other motion	no
majority	main, amend, appeal	no other motion	yes·•
two-thirds	debatable motions	no other motion	yes•
two-thirds	debatable motions	amend•	yes•
majority	main motion	amend,• vote immediately, limit debate	yes•
majority	main, amend	vote immediately, limit debate	yes•
majority	variable in form	subsidiary motions, reconsider	no
majority	main motion	vote immediately, limit debate	no
majority	no motion	specific main, subsidiary, object to consideration	no
majority	main, amend, appeal	vote immediately, limit debate, postpone definitely	no
majority	main motion	all subsidiary motions	no
majority	main, amend, appeal	no other motion	yes•
majority	main motion	amend	yes•
tie or majority	decisions of chair	limit debate, vote immediately, postpone temporarily or definitely	no
no vote	any error	no other motion	no
no vote	no motion	no other motion	no
no vote	all motions	none	yes•
two-thirds	no motion	no other motion	yes•
two-thirds negative	main motion	no other motion	no
no vote	main, amend	no other motion	no
no vote	voice votes	no other motion	no

• Restricted. • After change in parliamentary situation.

For Further Reading

• Baker, H. Kent, "Meeting audit: Planning for improvement."
AHGF, 1982, pp. 49-54.

• Bradford, Leland P., *Making Meetings Work: A Guide for
Leaders and Group Members.* La Jolla, CA: University Associates,
1976.
   Practical book based upon the insight and experience of one of the
most influential writers on group dynamics. Every serious-minded
leader of volunteer task-oriented groups should own this book.

• Lawson, John D., *When You Preside.* Danville, IL: The Interstate
Printers and Publishers, Inc., 1980.
   The chapters on "Parliamentary procedure made easy" and
"Formal leadership responsibilities" are especially useful in the
management of business meetings.

• Martin, William B., "When your meetings aren't meeting their
objectives." *Training/HRD,* December, 1980, pp. 27-37.

• Robert, Henry M., *Robert's Rules of Order Revised.* New York:
William Morrow and Co., Inc., 1971.
   Classic, most-used reference on parliamentary law, nationwide.

• Rosenblum, Jack J., "A structured format for improving
meetings." *AHGF, 1982,* pp. 121-123.
   Written especially for management staff meetings; applications
for improvement of any business meeting.

• Schindler-Rainman, E. and Lippett, R., *Taking Your Meeting Out
of the Doldrums.* La Jolla, CA: University Associates (Association of
Professional Directors), 1975.
   Guidelines, tasks, and examples of informal meeting management. Emphasizes human interaction, group participation,
openness of expression, and mutual responsibility.

• Sturgis, Alice F., *Learning Parliamentary Procedure.* New York:
McGraw-Hill Book Co., 1953.
   A self-instruction book to be used with *Sturgis Standard Code of
Parliamentary Procedure.* Gives purpose and proper use of each
kind of motion, explanations, practice projects.

• Sturgis, Alice F., *Sturgis Standard Code of Parliamentary
Procedure.* New York: McGraw-Hill Book Co., 1966.
   A fresh approach to parliamentary law. Easy to use; clearly states
the intent of motions; explains the "why" of motions; shows "how"
to phrase all actions. Based on court decisions and backed by a permanent advisory board of nationally-prominent parliamentarians.

17

Managing Conflict Between Members

Can you imagine a voluntary organization, committed to action and based on democratic ideals, existing without conflict? One big, "happy family" always seeing "eye to eye"? A group whose members hold all the same values and attitudes, and who always agree unanimously on what to do and how to do it? Wouldn't that be ideal? Don't you believe it!

Conflict--disagreement among the membership on goals, plans, activities, procedures--can be a source of group energy and creativity, when it is of the *constructive* variety. But in order to capture the good in conflict and utilize its energizing and creative potential, you must first defuse the sort of conflict which tends to misdirect and weaken organizational achievement and vitality. Neither ignoring disagreements nor "agreeing to disagree" sets the stage for united group action. It takes capable leadership to identify *destructive* conflict when it rears its ugly head, and neutralize it before it gets out of hand. "Know-how" in analyzing and managing conflict is an absolutely essential leader skill.

As troublesome as conflict may be to confront and work through, it must be resolved. Conflict can be a force for growth or for destruction; it is rarely neutral! Most group problems result not from conflict itself, but from the way it's handled. Let's examine the options that leaders have available to deal with this challenge.

AVOIDANCE　　To employ this option is to simply ignore the conflict and let it be. It may not seem worth the effort to resolve it, or to make it work for the good of the individuals involved, or the organization itself. At least, you might want to avoid it at the present and come back to it later when conditions are more favorable. On major issues, however, ignored conflict can lead to emotional tension,

misunderstanding, intolerance, or even worse. Avoiding conflict does not deal with it. A step in the right direction is to talk
the issue out, understand the real source of the disagreement,
and then agree to disagree. At least, this will uncork the
tension and get the issues on the table.

ACCOMMODATION   Accommodation is agreement
                         through yielding or conforming to
the positions of others; cooperation in an effort to create
harmony, even at the expense of your own ideas and values;
agreement in the name of peace and tranquility, knowing full
well that you don't entirely buy into it. Although they're not
famous for being creative, accommodators are sometimes
valuable in resolving conflict by using social tact and
diplomacy.

COMPROMISE   Compromise involves a search for a solution which is mutually acceptable, wherein each faction
sacrifices something the opposition wants. Everybody wins
something, but doesn't get everything. This may not be the
best possible solution for everyone, but it's not usually the
worst, either. People who compromise settle for ''the best
they can get'' rather than take the time working together to
find a solution everybody wants. Voting is a compromise:
those in the majority give and take until they please enough
voters to win. But the losers lose totally, often with feelings
of defeat, disappointment, hostility (''we'll get 'em next
time''), and non-support for the project or decision.
Compromise may be the only way to go when time is short,
or when total agreement is impossible.

COMPETITION   This is the offensive, aggressive
                   approach to conflict resoution. It is
especially attractive to those in power and authority who like
to ''get things done'' and ''win.'' It is exploitative, in that
it takes advantage of the opposition's weaknesses by
resorting to all sorts of strategies and tactics, many of which
are subtle and disarming. In a competitive situation there is

little listening, little information-sharing, and little interpersonal reasoning. Folks who favor this approach feel that committees and group discussions just slow down the decision-making, and that the group should go for "the best" goal or decision, as decided by a few (one?) leader(s). They sincerely believe that members want it that way.

In fact, *competitiveness* as a way to resolve conflict is generally seen as inappropriate and destructive by volunteers. It does have its place, however, when competitive teams work toward the same goals, or when the organization is under attack by outside forces.

COLLABORATION   Collaboration is a total-membership approach to conflict resolution that blends all the positive aspects of organizational operations: the democratic ethic, interpersonal communication, the "golden rule," and group problem-solving. In the collaborative mode, the group: (a) accepts the fact that there is conflict; (b) takes time for sharing of values, needs, interests, and resources; (c) discovers many possible solutions and weighs the consequences of each; (d) selects the alternative that best meets the needs and concerns of each member; and (e) forms a team to plan, implement, and evaluate the outcome.

Collaboration takes more time and requires more commitment than other leadership approaches to disagreement. It is, therefore, often reserved for those issues of greatest importance to the membership. It is also the way that (a) generates the most creative solutions; (b) gets the greatest membership support; and (c) produces the greatest amount of personal growth of members.

It should be clear that there is no single, "best" approach that will help leaders deal with every conflict situation. Each of those listed above has merit under particular conditions. It is up to each volunteer leader to develop the skills to use any of these five leadership responses to conflict; and the sensitivity to select the appropriate one(s) to achieve the most positive results.

Whenever a decision is of major importance and all-out support of the membership is needed, the outcome of the discussion should be a *consensus* reached through collaboration; a decision that every member will support to some degree. In this collaborative process, the presiding officer must encourage those contributions that reflect openness, clarity, and creativity, at the same time dealing firmly with behavior which is counter-productive to the goal of consensus. Here are some ways to keep it all together during such discussions:

1. Ask for a "straw vote" when you want to know to what extent people are in agreement. A show of hands will indicate those who are not satisfied with a particular solution. Be careful not to force premature commitments, however. A "public" vote *can* be hard to change!

2. Find areas of agreement, narrow the field of disagreement to the most basic elements, then clarify and analyze what is being said.

3. List problems in the order of their difficulty, then begin discussion with the *least* controversial. This will release tensions and defuse potential aggressiveness.

4. Form small "buzz groups" when you want to get quiet members to speak up (and take away the audience to which the "big talkers" like to play).

5. Brainstorm when you want a creative explosion of ideas in an atmosphere of absolute permissiveness. Chapter 15 gives the "rules" for this creative process.

6. Post (on a chalkboard or newsprint) all points made on a given topic (key reasons for and against) for all to see, when you want to keep discussion on the topic and to stifle repetition.

7. Appoint a recorder to list pros and cons (when a chalkboard or newsprint is not available), and have the lists read when you want to get back on the topic or discourage redundancy.

8. Ask for questions from the membership when you sense their confusion or frustration resulting from a poor or overlong presentation.

9. Ask questions yourself, when necessary.

10. Call on members who are likely to have creative alternative solutions when you feel the group is considering only traditional alternatives (especially those they're not really excited about and are not likely to fully support in the end!).
11. Reject motions to vote immediately (''the previous question'') when you believe additional collaborative discussion will lead to consensus. (The best way to do this is to ask the maker of the motion to withdraw it, explaining the importance of further discussion in bringing about a solution that *everyone* will agree to and support. Refer to Chapter 16 if you need procedural help.).
12. Form a committee when you feel the membership does not have adequate information and is not ready to make a decision. Review Chapter 14.
13. Call for a recess when you feel there's need for ''a break in the action'': to give members a chance to talk informally with one another, to talk with warring individuals yourself, to go after refreshments, or to go to the bathroom. You may wish to use buzz groups to work on the problem *during* recess also.
14. Postpone the whole thing to a later meeting, if you feel the additional time will bring about enlightenment, greater understanding, or the energy needed to put it all together to everyone's satisfaction.
15. Alternate speakers for and against an issue when consensus is impossible within the time available, or when the issue doesn't require total membership involvement or support. Then bring the matter to a vote. Be sure to give everyone the opportunity to ask questions before voting... always.
16. Compliment speakers for being brief and sticking to the topic when others tend to do just the opposite. This will let them know that brevity and relevance are what you're after.
17. Stop discussion when things get out-of-hand. Appeal to everyone to start listening to one another, and to ask questions when they don't understand or don't agree, rather than trying to ''out-shout'' one another.
18. Stop proceedings when any member interferes in any way

with another person's right to participate fully in the meeting. Appeal to the troublemaker's sense of fairness.

19. Invite the aggressor to present a *solution* to the question being discussed if s/he is a member and the disturbance seems to be related to the business at hand, not just "hooliganism." If you can handle it, invite him/her to come to the microphone for an *interview* (do not "turn over" the mike, however). This might reveal something significant to the goals of the meeting, and the troublemaker may learn how to contribute to the exchange in a productive manner.

20. Meet with individuals privately (during a called recess or between meetings) when they dominate a discussion unproductively. Appeal to their desire for shorter meetings, and try to point out that they are "turning people off" on a personal level rather than on the basis of the merit of their contributions.

21. If all else fails, call a troublemaker "out of order." Ask him/her to leave, or have the individual removed from the meeting if necessary. (Make sure in advance that you are prepared to carry out such drastic action before you attempt it; a failure to follow through successfully could be even more disruptive.)

22. Assign individuals special tasks during the meeting when they ramble and repeat themselves in discussion after discussion. Consider such appointments as "audio-visual aids coordinator," or as "back-up recorder" for the secretary, or as a special recorder of key points to be summarized when called upon by the presiding officer. Caution here: don't give disrupters a sense of "authority"--that could backfire!

23. Collaborate with individuals on the leadership team, and be creative with others who have definite organizational roles to perform, whenever there are overlaps and/or gaps in their duties. Interpersonal conflict is often caused by two people having different perceptions of what they're supposed to be doing. ("Who's in charge of this project, anyway?")

Volunteer organizations that thrive year after year build-in effective processes to ensure that members will hear and understand one another when there are disagreements. Conflict and disagreement are not signs of disloyalty; they are fuel for the pursuit of inquiry and excellence. There are two kinds of conflict...that which stimulates and energizes discussion, and leads to valuable and creative decisions, and that which feeds egos engaged in competitiveness and winning. Effective leaders have developed the skills to encourage *constructive* conflict and direct it for the good of all through the collaborative process. Democracy demands diversity, access to participation, open communication, and equal respect of self and others.

For Further Reading
• Benne, Kenneth D. and Muntyan, Bozidar, *Human Relations in Curriculum Change.* New York: The Dryden Press, 1951, pp. 302-353.

Conflict and creative opportunity, conformity and deviate views, conflict and methods of deliberation, and conflicting values, views, interests, and orientations.

• Cathcart, Robert S. and Samovar, Larry A. (Eds.), *Small Group Communication: A Reader.* Dubuque, IA: William C. Brown Co., Publishers, 1970, pp. 143-148.

"The role of conflict in discussion" stresses value of conflict in reaching decisions.

• Gulley, Halbert E., *Discussion, Conference, and Group Process.* New York: Holt, Rinehart and Winston, 1964, pp. 278-283.

Sources of conflict and methods of agreement.

• Simpson, Donald T., "Handling group and organization conflict." *AHGF, 1977,* pp. 120-122.

Conflict can be healthy if it is handled and resolved constructively. Methods include denial-withdrawal, suppression-smoothing over, power-dominance, compromise-negotiation, and integration-collaboration.

• Stepsis, Joan A., "Conflict-resolution strategies." *AHGF, 1974,* pp. 139-141.

Responses to conflict situations are generally avoidance, defusion, or confrontation. Confrontation can be treated as power or negotiation. Negotiation skills are discussed briefly.

• Wood, Julia T., "Constructive conflict in discussions: Learning to manage disagreements effectively." *AHGF, 1977,* pp. 115-119.

Excellent presentation of the need for confronting conflict openly in the pursuit of quality decisions. Managing conflict as a positive force includes a broadened understanding, increased alternatives, and membership interaction and involvement.

18
Keeping Records

Some volunteer organizations don't keep records at all and seem to get along just fine. If that's the way it is and all is well, why change?

Other organizations keep the bare minimum of records, usually in longhand, and stored in a notebook. These usually include the meeting date, call to order, president's report, financial report, and business transacted.

In both kinds of organizations, there is generally no parliamentary procedure to speak of and the meeting is likely to end informally, with refreshments, a program, or a party.

This chapter presents a system for those organizations that need to keep thorough records. Regardless of your past experience or current practice, you may want to keep reading; at least a few of these ideas may be helpful in your organization!

One of the most important administrative tasks of an organization is that of keeping official records of the group's business...concise, readable and accurate *minutes* of each meeting. During meetings, the secretary is usually so involved with keeping track of what's going on that it's seldom possible for him/her to get involved in discussions. The secretary works as a team with the president, following the agenda and taking complete notes. Although not necessarily an authority on parliamentary procedure, the secretary should know the basic principles so that the minutes are absolutely correct in that regard.

Note Taking

Complete, accurate notes taken during meetings are essential to being able to write good minutes later. This involves:
1. Being ready with all correspondence that may have to be read during the meeting.
2. Reading correspondence aloud, as directed by the president.

3. Reading the minutes of the previous meeting aloud, as directed by the president.

4. Listening to the content of a motion, writing it down, reading it aloud when requested, and getting feedback from the maker of the motion to be absolutely certain that it is correct before the president asks for a second. (This should also be done when motions are made in writing and given to the secretary.)

5. Recording the names of the maker of the motion and the second.

6. Informing the president if a motion does not have a second before discussion.

7. Being ready to respond to the president's request, "Will you please read the question?" ("The question" is always the exact wording of the motion *on the floor*.)

8. Recording the exact vote on all matters that require a two-thirds majority, and whenever a "division" or "roll call" is requested.

9. Having the membership list ready, to check for a quorum before the meeting is called to order, and to handle a roll-call vote whenever one is requested by a member.

10. Getting the signatures of all those present (if sign-in attendance is a standing rule or tradition of the organization).

11. Getting copies of all reports presented at the meeting, along with the name(s) of those who participated in the presentation.

12. Getting the names of all guests who make presentations. (It is sometimes important to get titles and affiliations, and perhaps a copy of the presentation as well.)

13. Recording the action taken by the group after each report or presentation.

14. Keeping track of time limitations on individuals or agenda items unless the president assigns someone else as "timekeeper."

15. Getting the names (sometimes the addresses, telephone numbers, and times available for meetings) of people who have agreed to carry out a task or to work on a committee.

Why Minutes?

A few words about the purposes served by the final and
official minutes of a business meeting are in order before we
get into how to write them. Minutes...
...are the official and legal record of the organization.
...inform members who could not attend about what
happened.
...help in following up on assignments and decisions.
...help in formulating the agenda for the next meeting.
...give continuity to the procedures and traditional activities
of the organization.
...are a valuable review of the activities of the past and aid in
report writing and formulating future activities and programs.
...are a valuable resource in selecting members for honors,
awards, nominations.

Preparing the Minutes

Official minutes vary somewhat with the nature of the organization, but these are generally accepted guidelines for
material to be included:
1. Name of group, type of meeting (general, regular, special,
continued) and place, date, and time of meeting.
2. The style and format of minutes should indicate major
agenda items by underlining or other identification along the
left margin. (Number the pages consecutively throughout the
year.)
3. Names of the persons present. (There are many variations
on this point, including voting members, non-voting
members, guests, absences, excused absence, proxies,
tardies.)
4. Quorum count, call to order and the name of the presiding
officer.
5. Correction and approval of the minutes of the previous
meeting (for substantive corrections, this should include the
name of the person who made the request).
6. The exact wording of motions, name of the maker (no nick-
names, please!), name of the seconder, and whether the

motion was passed or defeated. The exact vote is taken by "division" or "roll call." (Any member has the right to have the vote recorded in the minutes, upon request.) Sometimes "MSP" is shown to indicated "moved, seconded, and passed," and "MSF" to indicate "moved, seconded, failed." Example:

MSP Mary Smith/John Jones "that $100 be allocated for officer travel this year."

7. The exact wording and outcome of all subsidiary motions; e.g.: to amend, refer. Example:

MSF Bill White/Sandy Green "to amend the main motion by striking the word 'travel' and inserting the word 'expenses.'" (If "division" had been called, this might have been recorded as MSF 12-15, indicating that 12 "ayes" and 15 "nay" votes resulted from a hand vote.)

8. A record of the vote of any member who requests that his/her vote be entered in the minutes.

9. The exact wording of a committee assignment including any power to act, the date due and the names of the committee chairperson and members.

10. Incidental (procedural) motions such as *points of order, parliamentary inquiry* and *questions of privilege* are *not* shown in the official minutes unless they result in an action directly affecting the business transacted.

11. Main points made in debate are generally included in *committee minutes* (it helps in preparing the report and making recommendations), but *not* generally included in the minutes of an organization's business meeting, unless requested by a member and ordered by the president.

12. Be brief. Be specific. Be accurate.

13. Conclude your work of art with:*"Respectfully Submitted"*

(signature)
B. Brown, Secretary

Committee Reports

Meetings often include a number of committee reports. Some are simply "progress reports" and need not be entered in the minutes unless a change is made in the committee's task, authority, or budget. Others are final reports, and that's a different matter.

When reports are presented in writing, the secretary need include only the conclusions or recommendations in the minutes with a notation that the complete report is on file. The minutes must show the action(s) taken on the report by the membership.

When final reports of committees are presented orally, the secretary must gather the essentials of the report in every way possible so the minutes will be complete and accurate. It helps to have a tape recorder ready for such occasions. If all else fails, the last recourse is an interview with the committee chair after the meeting.

Records, Records, Records!

Most organizations maintain a file (sometimes a box) of minutes and committee records. Unless there is a central office or depository, such boxes are shuffled from secretary to secretary between terms of office. Treasurers have a similar responsibility with regard to financial records. Then there are newsletters, scrapbooks, plaques, trophies, photographs, and the organization's original charter and similar official documents. No one seems to know what to do with all this memorabilia, and no one *dares* throw it away! Maybe the leadership team should check this out and establish a suitable plan for this part of the organization's management.

As years go by and officer teams follow one another, the history of the organization becomes increasingly faded and forgotten except for the records filed away by secretaries, treasurers, and perhaps historians. Keep them well and dutifully; if *you* don't, you can bet that no one else will!

For Further Reading

• Sturgis, Alice F., *Learning Parliamentary Procedure*. New York: McGraw-Hill Book Co., Inc., 1953, pp. 276-282.

What minutes contain, form of minutes, correcting and approving minutes, committee meeting minutes, sample minutes.

19

Creating Good Programs

Whatever the nature of your organization, an occasional good program can change the pace of a meeting or spice things up a bit when heavy debate and decision making threaten to drag you down. Whether you have a program at every meeting or just once in a while, this chapter is meant to help you explore a wide range of ideas.

The basic considerations in program planning are *when* and *what!*

• Make up an "Events Calendar" for the entire year, noting such key *group dates* as regular meetings and elections. Add important *local dates:* celebrations, country fairs, festivals, shows, parades, exhibitions, athletic events, elections, school opening/closing and holidays; then include *state, national* and *international holidays:* elections, Mother's Day, Halloween, income tax deadlines, St. Patrick's Day, Valentine's Day, Veteran's Day, Youth Appreciation Week, the Super Bowl, the World Series... This will give a framework or grid so that you can look ahead for clues about possible programs.

• Analyze your organization's mission or purpose, and identify your *primary* commitments (e.g., "community service," citizenship, leadership development, legislation, the environment). Ask your program committee (or the entire membership) to "brainstorm" each primary purpose for programming ideas. The resulting large number of ideas can be reviewed and refined into potential programs for the year. Keep programs varied in whatever ways you can; try different locations, lengths, formats and contents from one meeting to the next. A series of information-only speeches is likely to bog down even the most scientific among us!

Maintain member interest and enthusiasm by including panels, dialogs, symposia, talks, forums, films, slide shows, field trips, live satellite-links to international experts, socials, game nights, workshops, equipment demonstrations, entertainment shows, picnics, barbecues, progressive dinners, art shows, dances,...*anything* appropriate to the purposes and interests of your group.

Strive for balance, of course. You can't be "all things to all members," but you will appeal to a broader base of membership if you offer more than the usual dry 30-minute speech after lunch!

Sources of Programs for Meetings

Seek program features television can't offer..."real people," like your members and local personalities... forum-related programs where your members can interact with the presenter and each other..."hands-on" experiences like the sight of a real art treasure, the taste of Leonard's chocolate-dipped insects, the smell of exotic plants or the feel of a live boa constrictor.

Start with your own members. They are easily available, and, getting to know one another in this manner is an excellent teambuilding experience. They won't necessarily be among the best speakers available, but it should be interesting, they will grow from it, and it's great for strengthening the future leadership fiber of the organization.

Try "Who Am I" talks by new members. Give them five minutes each and some specific ideas about what to say (highlights of your life, what you hope to get from your membership, your idea of a perfect vacation or job, what you'd like to be doing five years from now).

Build a panel, dialog, or symposium (with or without a forum attached) around one or more members. Bring in non-members to complete the program plan as needed.

Look for members who have had unusual experiences and feature them: "I Was There" (historical event, well-known news story, etc.), "People I've Known" (famous personalities, politicians, movie/TV stars, etc.), "Places I've Been" (adventures, unusual experiences), "A Funny Thing Happened to Me on the Way to..." (anything goes).

Local personalities and authorities are generally easy to find on just about any subject. Public and private agencies are generally glad to offer the names of experts; give a call to colleges and universities, medical centers, historical societies, museums, galleries, zoos, military bases, environmental groups, public safety agencies (fire, police, sheriff, highway patrol), public officials and legislators, volunteer agencies (American Red Cross, American Heart Association...), youth group leaders, consumer protection organizations, and many, many more. Look them up in the Yellow Pages.

The pool of available program presenters is so large and so diverse, the challenge is not to *fill* your calendar, but to design a *master plan* of what you want, and then go out and arrange it. Stick to your mission and purpose, balance entertainment with education and information, and blend some of them with traditional dates on the calendar.

Making the Most of Each Program

Give every program a title, and get agreement on it with the presenter. It is not very classy to announce a program as "Nancy's Trip Up The Amazon," or "Phil will talk about baking bread in his tailpipe oven." Try... "What To Do Before The Earthquake Quakes," "Breakfast Among the Boas," "The Other Side of The Hill," "How To Win Without Being Aggressive."

Take the initiative on titling a speech when talking with the prospective presenter. Assuming you know what the presentation will be about, have some catchy titles to suggest. Creative titles give speakers a precise point around which to build the performance *and* create interest and curiosity among your members.

A one-way speech alone seldom makes for a great program, especially when the purpose is educational or informational. In addition to audience participation, be prepared to supplement a talk with various kinds of visual and audio aids. Be certain that everyone can see and hear what's going on. Find out early in your term where you can arrange easy access to an *overhead projector,* an *opaque projector, 16mm film projector, videotape equipment, 35mm slide projector, microphones, and speakers.*

The creative uses of these audio-visual aids gives diversity to presentations, helps communicate detailed information, enhances audience involvement, and focuses attention to the topic before the group.

Care and Feeding of Program Guests

Every program presenter, regardless of experience at such things, needs certain information after saying "Yes" to an invitation. There are also some amenities that should be extended to make your guest's experience more enjoyable.

GUESTS NEED TO KNOW
IN ADVANCE

- Name of the Organization
- Where the meeting will be held (and how to get there)
- Date and time
- Name(s) and title(s) of others on the program (if appropriate)
- Where on the schedule (if there are others)
- General make up of the audience (interests, occupations, age range, children, etc.)
- Availability of audio-visual equipment
- Whether a forum is desired after the presentation
- When fee will be paid (it's best to have this in contract form, or at least in writing)
- Suggestions about what topic/subject to cover, and a *title!*
- *Exactly* how long the presentation will take (very important!) and how they will be informed when tme has expired.

Be sure to confirm all the above in writing promptly.

THE AMENITIES

- Meal(s)
- Overnight lodging (in a home or commercial establishment)
- Personalized transportation
- A host/hostess at the door to escort, help carry things, introduce to appropriate individuals, help them get seated.
- Copy of a photograph taken during the meeting or newspaper clippings covering the event, with letter of appreciation, following the appearance.

THE INTRODUCTION There are no absolute rules about how to introduce a speaker. In general, though, the more well-known the speaker, the shorter the introduction. And it is usually best to say no more about the speaker than that which is relevant to the topic. The process of ''launching'' a speaker is so simple there's no reason at all for fouling it up. First, *identify the subject;* Relate it to the audience and create a little suspense. Then *present the speaker;* tell why s/he speaks with authority on this subject, mention his/her position, and finally give his/her name.

Here's an example: "Ladies and Gentlemen: the place where we are seated tonight was once under the sea. I know many of you have discovered various kinds of shells in the nearby hills and have wondered how this area developed into such a pleasant place to live. You'll be glad to know that our featured guest can give us some answers to your questions about the history of our region, and perhaps a prediction of changes yet to come. Our guest has devoted a lifetime to studying the complex geologic history of this region, and telling its amazing story in books and on the lecture platform. She brings us a fascinating story, titled "The Mountains and Seas Around Us...Then, Now, and Later." I am pleased to introduce the noted scientist, author, lecturer, and Professor of Geology at the University of Cucamonga, Dr. Margaret Rockstory." Start the applause, and remain standing until the speaker is comfortably situated at the podium.

After the talk...lead the applause and give a brief expression of appreciation in behalf of the audience: "Thanks so much, Dr. Rockstory, for bringing us that very interesting and informative message."

The program team of your organization can "make or break" your meetings. Effective programming requires good planning in advance, a flair for imaginative ideas and resources, the ability to present them to the membership with style, and support from the full leadership team (including the funds needed to do the job!).

For Further Reading

• Author unknown, "Put punch in your program." *Nation's Business,* February, 1968.
    Simple, time-tested rules to assure success; written especially for the management of invited speakers.
• Sutherland, Sidney S., *When You Preside.* Danville, IL: The Interstate Printers and Publishers, Inc., 1964, pp. 59-67.
    How to invite, introduce, and use a speaker.

20
Getting Good Publicity

Who needs it? You do, whenever you're sponsoring a revenue-making event, you want the public to know about your events or services, or one of your members does something that deserves special recognition. Good publicity will enhance your visibility and attractiveness, a big help if you want to attract new members!

Publicity is different from keeping your own members informed. Publicity is directed to the *general public* (or to certain segments), and it is intended to cause a specific response. The key questions in designing a publicity campaign are: "Whose attention do we want to attract?" and "What do we want them to do?"

For example, if you're planning a major pancake breakfast fund-raiser, and you have arranged for a popular children's TV personality to perform, your target population is *families with children,* and you want the families *to attend.*

If, on the other hand, you need the support of the city council for a project, your target population is *city council members* (and perhaps their families), and you want them *to support* your use of a particular city park for your annual kite-flying contest.

Knowing your target population and what you want them to do makes it easier to choose from among a variety of publicity-getting resources and strategies. There is much to know about competing successfully for public attention. We'll briefly describe several different types of publicity techniques commonly used to let people know about organizations and their activities.

News Releases

They cost very little (duplicating expenses only, if you have a volunteer typist!) and can be a very effective way to reach the general public. The easier you make it for the newspaper copy editor, the better your chances of getting publicity. Although news people are primarily interested in public-interest events like an important guest speaker, a *factual* movie, an awards ceremony, a public service event, you'll be more likely to get coverage if you...

...Get the who, what, where and when in the first paragraph or two;

...Type your copy, double spaced, and keep paragraphs short;

...Stay away from glowing adjectives, long, fancy sentences and value judgments;

...Always include a name and phone number for further information — both in the article itself and elsewhere on the page.

...Send as many releases as there are media (newspapers, magazines, radio, TV) which cover your "target population."

Radio Public Service Announcements

Here's another approach which is both free and effective with the general public. These can also be added to their "Calendar of Public Events." Ask about it.

...Limit your copy to 30 or 60 seconds reading time.

...Place copy on 3 x 5 inch cards clearly labeled as "Public Service Announcement."

...Keep them simple, short, straightforward, and sweet.

...Put the name of organization in an easy-to-see spot on the card.

...Put an END DATE at the bottom...the last day it's worthwhile to broadcast it.

...Mail to PUBLIC SERVICE DIRECTOR, using the individual's name if you know it.

Newspaper Ads

Not free, but quite cost-effective on a local basis, such ads can be very effective with the general public.

...Select the *right* newspaper!

...Ask the newspaper's advertising representative about readership coverage to be certain the ad will reach the people you want to reach.

...*Column inches* is the basis for charges. An ad 3 columns wide and 3 inches deep is nine column inches. The width of columns varies from newspaper to newspaper; look through the newspaper of your choice, take column measurements, call for rates and you can figure the cost yourself.

...Consider classifieds if your paper has an "announcements" or "personals" column.

...The newspaper's staff will help you with the artwork if you choose a (more expensive) "display ad."

Radio Ads

These also cost money, but can be very effective with a local or regional audience.

...Select the right station(s)!

...Spots can be produced (taped) at the station, and the staff there will usually help you do it.

...Ads are usually 30 or 60 seconds in length.

...Ask each station about the characteristics of their listeners, that is, age groups, interests (they usually have extensive data on this).

...Cost is based on length, times of day, and number of times used.

Posters

Well designed signs and posters can be inexpensive and highly effective, when placed in locations where the people you want to reach will see them. A brainstorming session will probably generate a list of effective ideas (supermarkets, community centers, laundromats...).

Other Approaches to "Select" Publics

Publicity is a terrific opportunity to "turn loose" your most creative members. Try these, and more...
..."Flyers": in the mail or door-to-door.
...Personal contact (your members *should* be your best publicists!).
...Telephone campaign (the caller should know the receiver).
...3 x 5 cards in laundromats, supermarkets, and bus stations.
...Balloons and T-shirts.

Who Does All the Work?

Develop a publicity team. Include those members who like to write, take photographs, design and make posters, work with media personalities. It can be fun and perhaps an "easy-entry" for new members since there are such a variety of things that have to be done.

This is only the briefest thumb-nail sketch of the world of local publicity. Your best resources, if you want to be right "up-to-date" on all these media, are the local media personalities themselves. Your publicity team may wish to arrange to meet them personally and get acquainted so that any telephoning that follows will not be between strangers. Remember that all media are inundated with material and calls. Make yours unique to stand out from the crowd. The best way to do that is to prepare and present the material in a *businesslike, accurate,* and *attractive* manner. It's worth the effort!

21

Evaluating Your Organization

Evaluation is a process of analyzing the overall effectiveness of the organization, and it can be done with varying degrees of thoroughness. Which box best describes your organization's evaluation process?

- ☐ We don't evaluate at all.
- ☐ We talk informally about "how we're doing," but never put it on the agenda.
- ☐ We have oral and/or written reports on individual projects and activities with some membership participation.
- ☐ The leadership team evaluates progress on goals set at the beginning of the year and reports results regularly to the membership.
- ☐ Members are involved in a complete organizational self-study based upon our statement of purpose (mission) and our overall progress on goal accomplishment.

Why Evaluate the Organization?

• To provide the basis for reaffirming or changing the organization's mission and long-term goals;
• To analyze accomplishments and shortcomings in an effort to improve future planning;
• To demonstrate accountability to supportive members, friends, and affiliates;
• To appraise member satisfaction, changing interests, and readiness for new responsibilities or training;
• To examine the general quality of group processes (communication, meeting procedure, problem-solving, goal setting, and action planning); and

• To get feedback from selected individuals and other groups who are important to the organization's success.

   Some organizations relegate the responsibility for doing an annual self-study to the officers, to a committee, or to paid staff. Others invite everybody to participate. Good things happen when you choose a ''wide-open'' approach: members' feelings of ''ownership'' and self-worth are enhanced, and members involved will be much more in touch with the affairs of the organization.

   Groups that prefer simple evaluation formats tend to be small, informal, local, independent, and membership-financed. Organizations that opt to make evaluation a major annual project are usually large, affiliated, and dependent upon outside resources. These groups usually have major goals related to public service.

How, When, and What Do We Evaluate?

   All organizations have a *mission*--that basic ''something'' that brought the group into being. Evaluation ought to be a continuous process which looks at how well that mission is being carried out. Regular feedback about successes and shortcomings is invaluable in keeping the group on course toward its goals for the year. That is pretty idealistic, of course, and for most groups, a comprehensive end-of-the-year evaluation process is a more realistic answer to this important group function.

   As newly-elected officers get ready to launch into a new year, four questions need to be asked about the group they have ''inherited:''
• Where are we now?
• Where do we want to go?
• How do we get there?
• How will we know when we've arrived?
   Last year's evaluation is this year's starting point, answering the question: ''Where are we now?''

Let's assume that you're an officer in a progressive organization that values both the basics (mission, goals, and
resources) *and* human development. Here's a comprehensive
outline for an evaluation process with all members
participating:

1. The *Mission* is a general statement of purpose. It reflects
the values of the group that attract members, and establishes
group parameters within which goals are set. For example,
the Slippery Rock Arts Association declares that,
"Art, in all its forms, is vital to the quality of human exis-
tence throughout the world. It is our purpose to enrich the
environment of this community with music, art, crafts, dance,
and drama so that people of all ages may learn about, experience, and appreciate the worth of artistic endeavor."
*Does your group have a clearly-stated mission? Do your
members know and understand it? Have you discussed it
recently enough to be sure it affirms your purpose?*

2. *Long-Term Goals* are those commitments that extend for an
indefinite period of time, year after year. For example:

...Award two scholarships each year to graduating high
school seniors who have demonstrated unusual creativity
and talent in the arts.

...Sponsor an annual "Slippery Rock Gem and Mineral
Show" on the Fourth of July.

...Sponsor a renowned artist-in-residence for one week
each year at Slippery Rock College.

*Are your long-term goals consistent with your mission? How
effective are they? To what extent have members supported
them? Should changes be made?*

3. *Short-Term Goals* are programs, projects, and/or services
intended to reflect the interests of members during a given
year. Examples:

...Sponsor an entry in the county fair's "Bird-Whistling
Contest."

...Send a delegation to the County Board of Education to
protest reduced financial support for music in the schools.

...Sponsor a "Swap Meet of the Arts" to purchase a new
stereo system for the senior citizens' center.

Are your group's short-term goals consistent with your mission? With the long-term goals? Do members readily volunteer to see that short-term goals are achieved on schedule?
4. *Resources* include all those items that contribute to the net organization's worth. An evaluation of resources should include:

...Comparison of anticipated and actual income and expenses;

...Discussion of the cost effectiveness of various programs, projects, and services;

...Consideration of action needed to ensure fiscal strength over the long term and during the year ahead.

(Organizations that limit access to financial information to a few officers deny members information they need to participate fully in decisions that involve money.)

Are your organization's resources adequate to carry out your mission and goals? Are members fully informed about finances? Is there a membership-approved financial plan to foster fiscal strength? Are program planners required to account for expenses?
5. *Publications* include printed materials designed to attract members, to keep them informed, and to influence others. Members should know about and have a voice in decisions about all organizational publications, their purpose, actual use, and cost. These include:

...*Newsletters* to keep the membership informed.

...*Brochures* to attract members.

...*Pamphlets* to influence others.

...*Flyers* to make announcements to members.

...*Membership rosters* to help members communicate with one another.

Does your group have regular membership publications? Is there a team of members responsible for communications and publications? Are members regularly surveyed for ideas and opinions?
6. *Reaching Out* to develop relationships with other organizations, individuals, institutions and agencies can be essential to the achievement of goals. Few volunteer organizations

thrive entirely within themselves. Making contact to influence public policy is sometimes necessary to fulfill the organizational mission--perhaps even to keep the group alive!
Does your group make some contact with the larger community? Is there an effective advocacy campaign to support your mission? Do you regularly attempt to influence public policy on behalf of your goals?
7. *People*--including members, former members, prospective members, staff, the Board of Directors, and friends outside the group--are an organization's greatest strength. Skillful management of their experience with the organization is essential to their continued involvement and support. A complete organization evaluation should check out *their* perceptions of how things are going. Several sample questionnaires are included at the end of this chapter. Also review Chapters 7, 8 and 9 for some additional ideas in this area.
Don't overlook former members and prospective newcomers. Both may have something to contribute to your knowledge of member interest and satisfaction.
Does your leadership team regularly survey or interview or otherwise assess member satisfaction with the group? Do you have a systematic method to determine why members leave? Do you have an effective member recruitment effort? Are non-member "friends of the Association" invited to take part in your regular activities?
8. *Personal Development of Members* is an often unstated part of a group's mission. Some organizations continue year after year using ineffective and often destructive group processes, "turning off" some members, turning away others. Common areas of concern include communication, parliamentary procedure, conflict management, decision making, goal setting, action planning, and informal group discussion.Long-term membership development goals may be stated somewhere in the purpose or mission of the organization. New member orientation, officer training, regular member feedback "rap sessions," and leadership development retreats can be effective programs. Short-term membership development goals, to be accomplished within a

given year, may include such programs as a contest of knowledge about the organization, a skill-building retreat for interested members, a pre-nomination-for-office rally of "ballot hopefuls."

Does your mission statement include reference to the human values of the group? Is interpersonal communication encouraged and valued by your group procedures? Do members really feel they OWN this group?

Organizations that prosper are those that want to know how well they've done and how they might be able to improve for the future. The evaluation process should do just that, and it will have done it all when the process includes both task achievements *and* membership development.

MEMBERSHIP ANNUAL FEEDBACK

Using the following scale, put an "X" in the circle indicating your degree of satisfaction with what we have done as an organization during the past year. Use the extra space provided in the "Events" column to describe what you liked most, least, and what you would like to see changed.

Events	Very Dissatisfied									Very Satisfied
	1	2	3	4	5	6	7	8	9	10
Meetings	0	0	0	0	0	0	0	0	0	0
Service Projects	0	0	0	0	0	0	0	0	0	0
Team Work	0	0	0	0	0	0	0	0	0	0
Scholarship	0	0	0	0	0	0	0	0	0	0
Political Action	0	0	0	0	0	0	0	0	0	0
Newsletter	0	0	0	0	0	0	0	0	0	0
Recreation	0	0	0	0	0	0	0	0	0	0
Youth	0	0	0	0	0	0	0	0	0	0

SLIPPERY ROCK ARTS ASSOCIATION
Membership Involvement Questionnaire

1. Why did you join the Slippery Rock Arts Association?

2. What was done to get you started as an "informed member"?

3. How many people do you know by name?

4. How did you meet them?

5. How many people know you by name?

6. How did they get to know you?

7. When you joined, what did you hope to get out of the Association?

8. Who knows this? (#7)

9. What talents, skills, and/or energy do you have to offer the Association?

10. Is what you have to offer known by others in the Association?

11. What would make it easier for you to get more involved in the Slippery Rock Arts Association, meetings, and activities?

Any other comments?

Signed

SLIPPERY ROCK ARTS ASSOCIATION

A Survey of Publications

Please place an "X" in the column of
your choice and write comments in the
space below.

	Needs Major Changes	Needs Minor Changes	Perfect As Is
SRAA NEWSLETTER: A quarterly to keep members informed.			
SRAA BROCHURE: Information and application form to attract new members.			
SRAA PAMPHLET: General public information used to solicit donations for scholarships, etc.			
SRAA FLYERS: One-page notices of special events distributed to the public.			
SRAA MEMBERSHIP ROSTER: Annual listing of members, addresses, and phone numbers.			

Other suggestions and comments: _____
_____

Please sign _____

For Further Reading

• Lawson, John D., Griffin, Leslie J. and Donant, Franklyn D., *Leadership Is Everybody's Business.* San Luis Obispo, CA: Impact Publishers, 1976, pp. 151-162. (Out of print, but available in libraries.)
  Chapter 10, "Improvement through evaluation," covers meetings, events, goals and objectives, membership satisfaction, checklists, interviews, and suggestion boxes.

• Mill, Cyril R., "Reviewing objectives and strategies." *AHGF, 1983,* pp. 65-69.
  A structured exercise to review and evaluate the organization's accomplishments of the past year, to clarify and re-affirm the organizational mission, and to prepare objectives and action steps for major programs in the next year.

• Mink, Oscar G., Shultz, James M., and Mink, Barbara P., *Developing and Managing Open Organizations.* Austin, TX: Learning Concepts, 1979, pp. 169-177, 271-277.
  The evaluation process, the *CIPP* model of evaluation, process evaluation, product evaluation. Sample evaluation instruments.

• Pfeiffer, J. William and Jones, John E., *A Handbook of Structured Experiences for Human Relations Training,* Volume 3. La Jolla, CA: University Associates, 1974, pp. 22-30.
  Five instruments for group self-evaluation help a group evaluate its own functioning, provide a way to examine participation of group members, explore group norms.

Part 4

"Starting Anew"

The cycle of organizational life incessantly moves toward a change in leadership and the transition of responsibility from old officers to new. The manner of passing the gavel, the minutes, or the budget book is no less critical than the exchange of the baton between runners on a relay team. The process and timing must be done skillfully so that the responsibility for the next lap is clearly transferred. Then the cycle continues for your new leader to *LEAD ON*...starting with Chapter One.

Somewhere it must surely be written how many new volunteer organizations form every year. *LEAD ON* is written for the leaders of these groups, too, as evidenced by these final chapters. If this is your fortune,
READ ON!

22

Electing and Developing New Leaders

The best-managed election *ever* will not guarantee a great year if the most qualified candidates don't even appear on the ballot!

"Nominations are now open for the office of President." This phrase often signals the beginning of a well-known process to select new officers. In this approach, now's the time for any member to nominate any other member for president.

"I nominate Delores Austin for president."

"Thank you. Delores Austin has been nominated for president." The secretary takes notes on the record and someone writes Ms. Austin's name on the chalkboard, on newsprint, or on an overhead projector.

"Are there any other nominations for president?"

When all the names are in, the president states, "Since there are no further nominations for president, the nominations for this office are closed."

"Nominations for the office of treasurer are now open." "I nominate Jon Jingle for treasurer," and Jon Jingle responds, "I decline the nomination. I hate bookkeeping and can't even balance my own checkbook!"

Jon was neither interested nor qualified, illustrating why many organizations prefer to turn nomination process over to a committee. There are other reasons, too. A *nominating committee* can: determine in advance each prospective nominee's willingness to serve if elected; check on each nominee's qualifications; study the needs of the organization and distribute nominees to come up with a representative slate; prepare a list of potential officers who can work together harmoniously.

Nominating committees should be selected by the full *membership.* This is especially important in organizations which take officer elections seriously, and in groups which have certain factions likely to be critical of an appointed committee. In fact, it's probably best for the president to have no contact at all with the nominating committee until the actual committee report is presented.

If your membership is widely dispersed and difficult to contact directly, you may want to consider a membership questionnaire to determine their interests. There's a sample at the end of this chapter.

After the committee report is available, the president must open nominations for each office (one at a time) to permit members to nominate others not listed by the committee.

More About Nominations

• A nomination does not require a second, although a second is permissible if a member wishes to express approval of the candidate.
• In some organizations it is customary to preface the nomination with a speech about the qualifications of the nominee for office.
• A motion to close nominations is not out-of-order but it is unnecessary, and meaningless since another motion to re-open nominations can also be made.
• Unless the by-laws or standing rules state otherwise, it is legitimate for a nominating committee to recommend a slate of only one nominee for any or all offices.
• Members do not lose their right to be nominated by being members of the nominating committee.

Meeting the Candidates

Although you now have a slate of officer-candidates, and it's about time to vote, some members may not be acquainted with all the candidates. Here are four alternatives you may want to consider (set time limits!):
• Ask the candidates, one office at a time, to stand and make a brief statement of their qualifications, availability and their willingness to serve if elected.

• Permit a representative to introduce each candidate, to do the bragging, and to set the stage of humility for the candidate's message.
• After brief speeches by all candidates, allow an impartial panel to ask them questions.
• Allow each candidate an opportunity to meet with members of small groups.

When It's Time to Vote

Voting procedures are generally prescribed in the by-laws, but if not, any member may propose a motion to decide how it shall be done. There are two basic methods of voting: rising and ballots.

The rising vote, or show of hands, is used by very informal organizations immediately after nominations from the floor, so that those defeated for one office can be nominated for the next, until all offices are filled. This procedure presumes that all offices demand similar qualifications. Too often, unfortunately, even the most incompetent office-seeker can be elected to something as long as s/he "hangs in there" 'til the very end. Such practice offers little promise of an outstanding year for the organization (and it doesn't do much for the person who is defeated for one office after another, either!). A better alternative is to accept the nominations of a complete slate of office-seekers on the basis of their individual and collective interests and skills, and then to vote on them, one office at a time.

The secret ballot is the most valid elective process, since it eliminates the influence of peer pressure. Be sure the ballots are distributed carefully to avoid the possibility of irregularities, which could lead to a contested election. If the membership is widely dispersed, *mail ballots* may be the only method available. Here are some suggestions for mail ballot procedures:
• Include a fair and accurate assessment of each candidate's qualifications, or give each candidate equal space to prepare one.

• The ballot should be approved by the executive board before mailing.
• Indicate an absolute postmark deadline for ballots to be returned for counting.
• The secretary generally does the posting, making sure that every member receives a ballot, and absolute secrecy/privacy is guaranteed.
• A group of at least three tellers should count the ballots and report the results to the president.
• The results are generally reported to the membership by newsletter.

More About Elections

• The granting of power, or delegation of authority, to officers is done by members through the election process, and what is granted can be taken away (as provided in the by-laws).
• Secret voting by proxy, when another member casts the vote of an absent member, is out of order unless provided for in the by-laws.
• Some organizations conduct a run-off election of the two candidates getting the most votes when neither receives a majority on the first ballot.
• The legal vote cannot be made ''unanimous'' by passing a motion to that effect, although it is sometimes done to demonstrate popular support for the victor.
• Unless the by-laws state differently, a successful candidate assumes office as soon as s/he has been declared elected, or once the election results have been approved. Some organizations, however, do provide an installation ceremony of some kind.

Developing New Leaders

Whether to be intentional about developing new leaders or to let it ''just happen'' may be pretty well established within your organization. On the other hand, maybe no one ever considered the difference! Successful businesses certainly do not let new leadership "just happen;" they can't afford to. Management training at all levels is an integral part of the enterprise. Regardless of the position, volunteer leader or professional manager, all personal development comes from experience, regardless of whether that experience is intentional or accidental. Make your group's leader development an *intentional* experience!

Membership participation and involvement are advocated in every chapter of this book. We encourage all volunteer organizations to offer group experiences that encourage the personal growth of emerging leaders. For those members who seek challenging experiences that lead to greater leadership responsibility in the organization, we suggest you try a *retreat.* Ideas for such a program are included in Chapter 5.

Just as members come and go in the continuing life of an organization, officers are chosen from among them to carry out various designated roles. Members are prepared for future leadership responsibility by the quality and frequency of their group interactions; at meetings; during discussions; while doing committee work; and while at play. The more open, intense, and varied the experiences you provide, the more likely it is that leadership qualities will develop. Carefully planned leadership retreats offer an added dimension for those who seek intense personal group involvement. Whatever programs your group presents to prepare new leaders, don't rely on chance! (You may wish to re-read Chapter 5, *Building Your Leadership Team,* for more ideas on this subject.)

For Further Reading

• Lawson, John D., Griffin, Leslie J. and Donant, Franklyn D., *Leadership Is Everybody's Business.* San Luis Obispo, CA: Impact Publishers, 1976, pp. 139-145. (Out of print, but available in libraries.)
• Sturgis, Alice F., *Learning Parliamentary Procedure.* New York: McGraw-Hill Book Co., Inc., 1953, pp. 283-289.
  Nominations from the floor, nominations by committee, nomination committee report, closing nominations, voting, and the vote necessary to elect.

23

Passing the Gavel

What happens in your organization when there is a change of officers at the end of the term? It's not uncommon to have formal installation ceremonies, often at a banquet, a luncheon, or a regular meeting; including the passing of the gavel and listening to a series of speakers. But what about the behind-the-scenes exchange of information and records?

We have observed five general scenarios: the *Clean Sweep, Catch as Catch Can,* the *Inside Shuffle,* the *Fish Bowl,* and our favorite, the *Top-of-the-Line.* Here's how they happen; hopefully, they will give you some new ideas about how to make your organization's transition a little better.

The Clean Sweep

This is most likely to happen within semi-political organizations (such as student government associations) when one faction replaces another. In this case, the first order of business is usually to purge the files and records, and start over, from scratch. The motto becomes: "let's get organized." Traditions (some of them only one year old), long-term goals, standing rules and procedures are all thrown out in celebration of a "new era." Although this is certainly not a common occurrence in its most extreme form, it does happen to some degree in other kinds of organizations as well. The results, especially when terms of office are short, often have a devastating effect in terms of productivity and membership relationships. Rather than being a transition of leadership, this approach is much more like starting from zero. In a democracy, there are certainly more constructive ways to bring about change!

The "Catch as Catch Can"

This transition process usually begins with: "Why don't we (two) get together some time?" Picture this typical scene:

Leslie, the newly-elected newsletter editor, approaches John, the editor who is leaving office...

"John, I hope you can help me get started, I've never done anything like this before!"

"Don't worry about a thing, Leslie, I've got four boxes of stuff for you."

"Yes, but..."

"I'll drop them off at your place on my way out of town."

"You're leaving town?"

"Yep! Got a great job in Boonville."

"But, I've never edited a newsletter and I thought you'd..."

"It's simple. I'll write you..."

"Yes, but..."

"Bye, Leslie...don't worry about a thing.!"

Leslie needs more than a moment of silence! She needs some time with John...some "Chapter 3 quality communication." Not only is the above scenario a problem for Leslie, it is unfair to the membership and the organization. Furthermore, this "catch as catch can" method, even when done thoroughly, leaves the president and other officers totally in the dark about the future and functions of every office in the organization.

The Inside Shuffle

Some groups transfer information, records, and paraphernalia between pairs of incoming and outgoing officers at the end of the last meeting or at a special get-together for old and new officers between meetings. How thoroughly it is done is not known by others present...they are involved with their own concerns. This system does provide every new officer an opportunity to start out the term informed. But it *does not* provide all members of the new leadership team with all the

information needed to start thinking *teamwork.* Before the
session is over, there should be a *general* discussion, when
important questions can be discussed openly and a sense of
the overall leadership picture developed.

The Fish Bowl

This transition process is similar to the *Inside Shuffle,*
except that each pair of incoming and outgoing officers sits
facing one another in the center of a large circle of all others
present. The two carry on their information giving and questioning dialog so all can hear. When the dialog is over, others
can join in with whatever is on their minds...further suggestions, questions, clarification, and best of all, comments about
linkages and interdependence between other functions. New
officers get to know one another better, and they begin to
sense the value of teamwork during the term ahead.

Top-of-the-Line

An extended retreat experience of one or more days and
nights may be a luxury only a few organizations are able to
afford (both in time and money), but it should be given serious thought if your organization is serious about accomplishing goals and satisfying the membership.

The atmosphere of a retreat is described in Chapter 5 as
an invigorating environment for developing new leaders. It's
also ideal for being thorough about the transfer of responsibility from one team of officers to another.

The general format, site arrangements, and schedule of a
transition activity should be worked out well in advance.
(Some groups even make a pledge of retreat attendance a pre-
condition for running for office.) Primary responsibility for
planning, selling, and conducting the sessions should rest
with the outgoing officers, possibly with help from a consultant if interaction among all officers is desired (or if information and orientation material can best be presented by a third
party).

Consider the following when planning the program:
1. Historical perspectives of the organization...documents, policies, procedures, and officers' job descriptions.
2. Review of past goals, projects and activities...describing both successes and failures.
3. Resources available to officers...organization friends and foes, program ideas, how to get "things."
4. Financial procedures, a year-end fiscal summary, and a projection of future expenses and revenues.
5. Roles and relationships among the officer team and others outside the organization.
6. Skill-building sessions and leadership development training.

Finally, consideration should be given to the new officers' need to spend time together as they begin to build a team to work together during the term ahead. In some cases, it may be appropriate for the first part of the schedule to include both old and new officers, then to leave the new officers to themselves for a half-day or so to pursue the goals of team-building mentioned in Chapter 5. See the special briefs on "The Retreat Experience" and "So You Want to Hire a Consultant-Facilitator!" at the end of Chapter 5.

The change of leadership at election time can be traumatic in the life cycle of an organization. The process may range from no process at all, to whatever process the two groups think of or arrange to do at the "last minute," to a well-planned, comprehensive program. In the interest of stability, continuance of mission, traditions, long-term goals, we suggest that the transition process be stated in the by-laws or standing rules, or that it become a tradition in itself, written and followed year after year.

For Further Reading

• Lawson, Leslie Griffin, "Leadership transition." Columbia, SC: National Entertainment and Campus Activities Association, *Programming Magazine,* April, 1981, pp. 64-67.
   Pre-election activities, nominations and elections, post-election activities, and transition format.

24

Starting a New Volunteer Group

Groups form because members believe they can collectively fulfill some need that individuals cannot achieve alone. There is satisfaction from learning, or sharing, or doing something with others. Some groups are started to satisfy a temporary need, such as getting someone elected to public office, advocating a ''yes'' vote on a particular ballot measure, or improving the quality of life in one's neighborhood. Others are meant to function indefinitely. Although there are similarities in getting temporary and permanent groups started, there are also significant differences. Let's consider both.

Forming a Temporary Group

Assume your city was chartered ninety-eight years ago and folks are starting to talk about celebrating its 100th anniversary in some way. What to do? How to get started? What are the ''preliminaries''? The following are necessary steps:
1. Invite all those who might have some responsibility for getting things started to a planning meeting, at which you will agree on the purpose of the group, make arrangements for the first meeting (place, date, time, invitations, public announcements), select a temporary chairperson and a secretary, and draft a statement of purpose for the group. Here's one:
   ''It is agreed that this assembly shall form a temporary association for the purpose of celebrating the one-hundredth anniversary of the founding of the City of Pismo Beach, California. A president, secretary, and finance committee shall be elected to serve until the end of the celebration. This statement, signed by all persons present, shall be sent to all newspapers, radio and television stations in the tri-county area.''

2. Send invitations and arrange for public announcements of the general meeting through all area media.

3. Hold the first general meeting; at which a designated person from the organizing group should welcome all present, explain the purpose of the meeting, and conduct the election of president, secretary, and treasurer. After the election, the new president, secretary, and treasurer should take office and continue the meeting. The statement of purpose should be presented, amended if necessary, approved, and signed by all present. Get others involved right away by soliciting individual interests and ideas, and forming task committees. Before adjourning, be sure to make plans for the next meeting.

Forming a Permanent Organization

There are other citizens of "Pismo Beach" who are more interested in sailing than in city celebrations. Some of these folks have boats, others do not. Some are expert sailors, others are just learning, still others only watch and wish. But they've all talked about boats, sail care, buying, selling, racing, weather...

"Why not start a club?" "Yeah, I know some boat owners who would join!" "And some who don't have boats but who wish they did!" "We could give lessons." "We could have our own regattas." "But how do we do it?"

Those most interested in getting the organization started can get together and carefully lay out some plans for a first meeting. Their first few steps are very similar to those their civic-minded neighbors took to start their temporary group. Because of the continuing interest, the sailors' process inevitably gets more involved.

Here are important considerations to be addressed by your "steering committee":

1. What is the *purpose* of the organization? (buy boats? teach sailing? sponsor regattas? compete with other clubs? have parties?)

2. Will you affiliate with other organizations? (local, state, regional, national, international)?

3. How will the organization be financed (dues, sailing lessons, boat shows, donations, loans)?
4. What basic policies are needed (use of boats, boat damage, scheduling, reporting, safety)?
5. Shall the club be incorporated? (State non-profit corporation laws require certain rules of operation, and provide officers certain liability protection.)
6. Will there be more than one type of membership? (regular, associate, life-time, honorary)?
7. Will there be a limit on the number of members (member-boat ratio)?
8. How should members be selected (level of expertise, member sponsorship, boat ownership)?
9. Who is eligible to become an officer and how will people be elected (boat owners, sailing expertise, experience)?
10. What committees will be needed to run the organization (finance, boat maintenance, training, racing, membership)?

When these questions have been thoroughly discussed and answered, a committee should draft a set of by-laws (If you decide to incorporate, the by-laws *must* conform to the laws of the state. Check your local library for information if you don't have an attorney in the group.)

Make your by-laws a *single document* (rather than a "constitution *and* by-laws.") Set forth all the rules under which the organization will operate. It may help to "borrow" the by-laws of a similar established organization to get a general overview of one that (apparently) works. Don't simply adopt theirs and expect it to work for you.

Draft a resolution in advance of the first meeting for presentation to those in attendance. This is a special kind of motion which authorizes the formation of a permanent organization. "I move that those present form a permanent organization to be known as the Pismo Beach Sailing Club."

The First Meeting

The organizing group is responsible for the formative phases of the first meeting. This includes finding a place to meet, inviting interested people, greeting them upon arrival, helping them get acquainted with one another, calling the meeting to order, giving a background explanation of what's been done so far, outlining the plan for the meeting, presenting the resolution for discussion and approval, presenting the by-laws for discussion and approval, and conducting the election of new officers according to the by-laws. At that point the permanent organization is formed and the newly-elected officers take over.

The proposed by-laws may be read a second time in their entirety, article by article, discussing and amending as necessary. Finally, a motion should be made and seconded to adopt the by-laws (as amended). (Majority vote prevails.) To maximize understanding and participation, and to save time, each person present should be given a copy of the proposed by-laws in order to follow along, take notes, and support the final product. If it sounds a bit tedious ("I'd rather be sailing!"), think of it as an investment in *member-ownership* of your new group!

Most prospective members who come to the first meeting *are*, after all, interested in sailing (or poetry, or cooking, or community service), *not* writing resolutions and by-laws. Try to have as much of the "paperwork" as possible done in advance for their consideration and approval.

This is the "anchor chapter" of *LEAD ON.* If you have read it first because you wanted to know about STARTING A NEW VOLUNTEER GROUP, you're off to a good start! Now...go back to Chapter 1 and *READ ON* to find out more about "Tuning Up" for the job ahead (Part I), "Getting Started" (Part II), and "Getting Results" (Part III). Later, when you're ready to "pass the gavel" (or the key to the boat locker) to new leadership, you'll find Part IV right up the main channel. Good luck!

For Further Reading

• Robert, Henry M., *Robert's Rules of Order Revised.* New York: William Morrow and Co., Inc., 1971, pp. 284-292.
The first meeting (invitations, preliminary steps, selection of temporary chairperson and secretary, resolution to form organization), the second meeting (by-laws presented, adopted and signed, election of permanent officers).

• Sturgis, Alice F., *Learning Parliamentary Procedure.* New York: McGraw-Hill Book Co., Inc., 1953, pp. 215-220.
Temporary and permanent organizations, planning for a new organization, places for the first meeting, managing the first meetings, and resolutions to take action.

Index